# From Aristotle to Cognitive Neuroscience

Grant Gillett

# From Aristotle to Cognitive Neuroscience

palgrave
macmillan

Grant Gillett
Dunedin School of Medicine
University of Otago
Dunedin, New Zealand

ISBN 978-3-319-93634-5      ISBN 978-3-319-93635-2   (eBook)
https://doi.org/10.1007/978-3-319-93635-2

Library of Congress Control Number: 2018948151

Cover illustration: Pattern adapted from an Indian cotton print produced in the 19th century

This Palgrave Pivot imprint is published by the registered company Springer Nature
Switzerland AG
The registered company address is: Gewerbestrasse 11, 6330 Cham, Switzerland

# PREFACE

This book examines the nature of the human soul from an Aristotelian perspective by accepting that human beings have souls as part of their nature (which includes second nature or social and ontogenetic properties). I was persuaded to a form of Aristotelianism by my D.Phil supervisor at Oxford University—Cathy Wilkes and have found it a convincing framework within which to approach ethical and philosophical issues focused on human cognition and ethics. It is no accident that forms of Aristotelianism provide a philosophical foundation for developed biological, psychological, and medical science and also for certain strands of theology, and this book seeks to unpack why that is so. Many people have helped me to develop the manuscript as colleagues and mentors: Rom Harre, Derek Bolton, Carl Elliot, Hilde Lindemann, Jamie Nelson, John McMillan, Carl Mika, Charlotte Paul, David Green, Dirk De Ridder, Elana Brief, Alan Torrance, Giles Newton-Howes, the philosophy department at Otago University, colleagues in the Bioethics centre at Otago Medical School and elsewhere, and the many excellent students with whom I have had the privilege to work; some of whom have become notable scholars in their own right: Drew Donnelly, Lynne Bowyer, Claire Amos, Brent Hyslop, Deborah Lambie, Deb Stephens, Katherine Hall, Kati Taghavi, Simon Walker, and Jeanette Wikaira.

Scholarship is a joint endeavour, and like any human enterprise, it has its tensions, rivalries, friendships, collaborations, and collegiality, but a book such as this enables one to honour the many who have impinged on one's life path in a way that makes the academy what it is. It is they whom this preface seeks to acknowledge along with those notable forebears without which any scholarly endeavour can have no substance. ...

Dunedin, New Zealand                                                    Grant Gillett

# CONTENTS

# LIST OF FIGURES

# CHAPTER 1

# Introduction: Second Nature and Naturalism

**Abstract** Aristotle's account of the soul differs from Cartesianism; while it holds that the soul denotes a conception of a human being as not merely a physical or material thing, the division is conceptual and not in terms of a different metaphysical substance and it concerns the form of human life as self-organised, rational, and moral beings in a shared world using shared cognitive tools. The human soul animates and gives coherence to our lives and it develops, in part, through education to create a second nature developed out of the (first) nature human beings are born with. The account is extended by Kant and the phenomenologists who examine how human beings train their children as cognitive apprentices.

**Keywords** The human soul • soul and *psyche* • Neural adaptation • Human uniqueness

> *Then he stood before the fire, and looked me over in his singular,*
> *introspective fashion.*
> *"Wedlock suits you," he remarked. "I think Watson that you have put on*
> *seven and a half pounds since I saw you."*
> *"Seven," I answered.*
> *"Indeed, I should have thought a little more. Just a trifle more, I fancy,*
> *Watson. And in practice again, I observe. You did not tell me that you*
> *intended to go into harness."*
> *"Then how do you know?"*

© The Author(s) 2018                                    1
G. Gillett, *From Aristotle to Cognitive Neuroscience*,
https://doi.org/10.1007/978-3-319-93635-2_1

*"I see it, I deduce it. How do I know that you have been getting yourself
very wet lately, and that you have a most clumsy and careless servant
girl?"
"My dear Holmes," said I, "this is too much. You would certainly have
been burned, had you lived a few centuries ago."*

The human soul, a concept that indicates the uniqueness and moral significance of each human being, is a topic that philosophy has struggled with since Descartes. The Cartesian solution was radical: to posit two metaphysical types of substance, one of which was extended, mechanistic, and causal in its workings and one of which was immaterial, and the source of distinctly human nature. But there was always an alternative which located human beings squarely in the natural world but gave them a unique role as co-constructors of that world. That added complexity to their natural adaptation because, in part they were world-makers and self-makers unable to be studied like other objective phenomena. As self-organising and self-making systems, human beings imposed on the world and themselves certain meanings and values which transformed morally inert mechanism and an exploration of wheels within wheels into a different kind of enterprise—a moral science. The present work lies within the alternative strand of thought that originates with Aristotle. It traces human growth, development, and adaptation in a way parallel to that of a natural organism and is therefore broadly naturalistic. It ties that understanding to an evolutionary neurology that acknowledges our co-construction of the world; within that account, it looks at neurocognitive disruptions in what we make of ourselves. It locates value in that complex moral project and espouses an account of human freedom that avoids the metaphysical extravagance of dualism. Within such an Aristotelian enterprise one can argue for the reality of the moral community and even for a robust and natural conception of human spirituality.

Aristotle notes that human beings develop, in part, through education and argument and create in themselves a second nature based on the attributes they are born with. Sherlock Holmes is a case in point. Inference and causal reasoning, broadly human characteristics elaborated from our animal cognitive equipment through practice and argument, exploit a body of knowledge that is dynamic and in perceptuo-motor engagement with the world informed by shared learning and communication about a domain of interest. Being the world's greatest detective requires extensive self-formation using both types of experience.

*Second* nature builds on training and argument and transforms *first* (biological) nature to make a human soul (or *psyche*) a being-in-the-world-with-others. Aristotle's embodied theory of cognition places human beings in a natural environment, where they combine perception, action, and reasoning in the work of self-formation (autopoiesis). In so doing, they progressively configure their neural networks to achieve well-being in ways fitted to a human group within a given culture.[1] A culture develops certain techniques suited to human ethology and its cooperative mode of life.[2] The human *psyche* therefore integrates two modes of adaptation: causal/physical adaptations based on biological processes that *couple* its functions to an environment (as in embodied cognition theory), and discursive skills, obeying norms conveyed in an intersubjective domain where symbols are used in communication to mark the things we discern and the techniques we learn. Human growth therefore fits us for a context both through individual learning history and communication with others so that a human global neurocognitive workspace prominently incorporates shared circuits of cognitive activity (Hurley, 2008) tied to truth (through argument) and praxis through mimicry, cooperative techniques, and reciprocity with others.[3] Our cognitive skills, shaped in that way, are therefore inherently interpersonal and political, formed within human institutions and the symbolic order as part of a unique cognitive niche.[4] The complex processes of engenderment and connection producing human second nature distinguish us from other animals because we occupy "the space of reasons" (McDowell, 1998; Sellars, 1997), where we give an account of ourselves and justify our actions, an enclave within the natural world with its own forms of *poiesis* (or making) and necessity (or normativity, some of which rest on "oughts" rather than on brute causal interaction).[5]

Second nature, because human self-making under rational constraints is involved, seems to resist a purely naturalistic analysis. A naturalistic account aims to show how second nature emerges (in an anti-reductive manner, as noted by Kant (CJ, 217ff)) from physiological or neural connections, as revealed by neuroscience, in a top-down self-organising neural network integrating individual learning with the influences of a socio-political domain in which "oughts" are conveyed by discipline, training, and argumentation. This higher adaptive form of human self-formation (*autopoiesis*) produces a form of cognition that embeds the dynamic flux of ongoing embodied human life and cognitive maps supplemented by symbol-encoding structures so that semiotics (the need for interpretive approaches to symbol systems and symbolic processes) and discursive analysis—which pays attention to our positioning in networks of communication and power—must inform a synthesis drawing on both analytical and continental philosophy and non-linear neural dynamics (Freeman, 2000). That synthesis outstrips the resources of most varieties of physicalism (usually of a C17th, "Victorian," or mechanistic type),[6] but it resonates with Kant's analysis of natural teleology and the later Wittgenstein's deconstruction of philosophical concepts and categories in terms of grammar and the rules governing meaning).[7]

Human thought and consciousness draw on integrated neural assemblies forming a dynamic neural workspace responsive to self, the world, and discourse, effectively creating a triply influenced system combining language, argument, and self-positioning with sensori-motor coupling to the world[8] as it attunes a human being to a cognitive (ecological/ethological) niche through cerebral synchrony and integrates multi-level neural interconnections that form a dynamic and non-linear neural underpinning for cognition and consciousness (Freeman, 1994).

The human *psyche* (or soul) integrates and controls human behaviour as it emerges from a human being's situated trajectory within a domain co-constructed with others (Tomasello, 2014). In doing so, information that symbolism, reason, and argument make available to the predictive brain (Friston, 2010)[9] equips us better to deal with the slings and arrows of outrageous contingency through shared circuits of cognitive processing.[10] The resulting skills coordinate visceral, sensori-motor, emotive, intersubjective, aesthetic, intentional, ethical, and political activity into a multi-stranded and dynamic way of somatic being crafted to meet a variety of demands and constraints from one's engagement with others and with "cruel" nature, *in the raw*, as it were (Damasio, 1996). This integrative work is crucially mediated by ventral prefrontal areas of the human brain, and enables "skilful coping" (Dreyfus, 2014) in a domain of adaptation where, even if neural or psychological disruptions and fragmentations occur, those challenges to our harmonious being-in-the-world-with-others can be understood.[11] Seeing the brain as integrating diverse types of information (Hughlings-Jackson, e.g. 1887, p. 29), all of which are used by human beings to bring forth (Chemero, 2009) a co-constructed world that sustains them, offers a naturalistic route to understanding the soul, consciousness, and human value.

Second nature, an Aristotelian key to the human soul, links human ontogeny, language use, and cognitive neuroscience in an understanding of personal identity, free will, and philosophical psychology that draws on accounts of rule-following and intentionality to analyse human *autopoiesis* (self-formation).

Evolutionary neurology invokes top-down integration by the human organism of its own neural network to develop a non-Cartesian moral science of embodied cognition that acknowledges the discourses of humanity as they "bring forth" objects for consciousness from our engagement with the world to which we adapt ourselves.[12] Neurocognitive structures responsive to objects within their human contexts are based in shared forms of life that can be extended to new contexts.[13] Human "self-organising, autonomous, autopoietic activity in the world"[14] is engendered by second nature. It constructs integrating neural assemblies that represent and re-represent (and re-re-represent) the world (Hughlings-Jackson) through progressively complex dynamic perceptuo-motor cycles, forming the cognitive maps that allow triangulation (two subjects focusing on and communicating about the same thing), joint action, and higher-order conceptualisation of our dealings with things.[15] A human subject is therefore related to the world in a complex, triply responsive way: to self and the body, to the world in which one lives and moves and sustains one's being, and to propositional structures abstracted from human discourse. That triple responsiveness is non-linear and dynamic and elaborates "acquaintance"[16] by using discourse to mediate and help organise "information links" (Evans, 1982; Gillett, 2014b) between human subjects and the world.

This essay draws heavily on the history of neurological theory, contemporary neuroscience, and cognitive development as theorised by John Hughlings-Jackson (JHJ), Lev Semyonovich Vygotsky, and Alexander Luria. Each noted the internal relations between the human soul (or *psyche*) and nature in ways that are partly captured by contemporary embodied cognition theory as it delineates the active use of a global cognitive workspace which, for human beings, is informed by discursive encounters that shape propositional content or "propositionising" (through concepts and the rules governing them). Thus human beings must be seen in two registers: one arising from sensori-motor coupling or cycles of perception-action and the other closely linked to language and culture.[17] This duality is, however, naturalistic, and finesses the problem of connecting "representation" to reality because human subjects meld the two patterns of connection together in a predictive exercise (of modified anticipation that enhances perceptuo-motor cycles by using semantic "webs" of symbolism and "belief").[18] Non-human animals respond to the responses and predicted responses of other animals' behavioural control, but human discourse introduces explicit and symbolically mediated inference and offline (not directly engaged in current adaptive activity) elaboration of cognitive maps through reason and argument to "up their game." Aristotle indicates this extra dimension when he notes that the human intellect supplements animal cognition by thinking which obeys rules of truth and falsity (DA, 427b). His remark prefigures Kant's claim that thought using concepts is built on the active use of reason and is therefore discursive (CPR, B93). Discursive naturalism (Harre & Gillett, 1994) incorporates these elements to characterise the human soul as a product of human ontogeny in which mastery of the semantic and conceptual skills used by a human group organises perception, cognition, and action to fit their communal account-giving.[19] Studying that whole process is, therefore, a moral science.

This line of thought embeds a kind of existentialism whereby human subjectivity is enmeshed in the (surd) contingency of bodily life but inflected by the nuances and resonances of intersubjectivity. Cartesian thought is unrealistic in its cognitive individualism evident, for instance, in such problems as the "poverty of the stimulus" argument in linguistics and the philosophy of language whereby the child is conceived as a "scientist in the crib" rather than located within a praxis where people are interweaving language with their general getting along together, communicating and connecting with each other (Bruner, 1990, p. 70).[20] Appealing to triangulation, norms of communication, and shared praxes of instruction and correction (as in the later Wittgenstein, e.g. PI, #208) yields an account of the growth of the soul based on assembling shared circuits in a multi-layered neural network.

If life as it is lived is rendered in terms of communicable texts about what we encounter so as to form a storied or edited (digestible) form of real-time experience (Dennett, 1991), then representations actually re-present by transforming the causal impressions of the real world and its contingencies by using an overlapping set of cognitive maps grounded in actual states of affairs but also by exploiting words and their meanings (PI, #95) which make connections other than those evident in the actual situation (so thought can be of what is not the case (PI, #95)). Hence the absurdity of a map with "the scale of a mile to the mile" ... "we now use the country itself, as its own map, and I assure you it does nearly as well."[21]

Jorge Luis Borges' "On Exactitude in Science" describes the tragic uselessness of the perfectly accurate, one-to-one map:

> In time, those Unconscionable Maps no longer satisfied, and the Cartographers Guild drew a Map of the Empire whose size was that of the Empire, coinciding point for point with it. The following Generations, who were not so fond of the Study of Cartography saw the vast Map to be Useless and permitted it to decay and fray under the Sun and winters.
>
> In the Deserts of the West, still today, there are Tattered Ruins of the Map, inhabited by Animals and Beggars; and in all the Land there is no other Relic of the Disciplines of Geography.

The mistake of predicating of human life and its encounters what lies in our methods of representing them (PI, #104) fools us into thinking that the human soul and its capacities obey causal constraints of neurophysiological time in terms of their content—what we are thinking about or experiencing rather than just the vehicles employed (the neural processes allowing that mental activity).[22] But the contents of our stories and meaningful experiences are both narratively and physiologically connected and obey discursive rules configured partly by reason into a coherent conscious life. The underlying neural processes may seem chaotic in their own terms or, at best, non-linear and dynamically complex in perplexing ways, but there is another entrée into understanding them (Freeman, 1994; Dennett, 1991). In studying the soul and human consciousness we "look awry" from a different conceptual framework because consciousness as lived (or from within) is a mixture of contingency, association, and raw existence and abstractions edited for storytelling and symbolic or meaningful exchanges, satisfying the constraints and desiderata of the accounts we give of ourselves.

Therefore an adequate philosophical account of human thought and consciousness—the core functions of the human soul—is, we could say, as follows: (1) it is apt for reasoning and analysis, (2) it should dovetail with our understanding of nature and human evolution, (3) it should show how cognition and consciousness put us in touch with reality (as triangulated and communicated about), (4) it should explain why our nature as "critters" is important to our being souls of a human type, and (5) it should explain the link between soul and value as the basis of conscious participation in a community of ends (Cranford, 1988; Levy, 2014).

## 1    RECAP ON CHAPTER 1: FIRST AND SECOND NATURE— LIVED EXPERIENCE AND MEANINGFUL LIVES

Naturalism is usually taken to be a form of explanation more or less equivalent to a mechanistic causal materialism, but both Aristotle and Kant think that mechanistic reading distorts our view of human beings. Organismic purposes and causal contingency as a proper basis for understanding the natural order usher on to the stage something other than mechanism, and that expanded conception of naturalism is expanded again when we consider human adaptation to a social order in which things take on a certain "shape" in the stories we construct about ourselves and our world. *Second nature*, an elaboration of purely biological nature, grows out of human biology to fit us for that distinctly human level of adaptation, and it is a joint product of natural causality and discourse, the origin of meaning. Life takes on meaning as we learn the skills of accounting for ourselves as beings-in-the-world-with-others. The human soul is therefore the focus of moral science as we make of ourselves beings that are attuned, as we should be (to echo Kant), to a shared world. The human nervous system is exquisitely suited for realising this attunement, and studying its subtleties takes us from Aristotle to consciousness and intentionality as a human mental life takes shape.

### NOTES

1. Discussed in Chap. 3 on evolutionary neurology.
2. R. Harre and G. Gillett, *The Discursive Mind*, 1994.
3. The link to truth and falsity is found in Aristotle (DA, 47b15) and Frege (1977, p. 4), and the link to praxis is both Aristotelian and post-structuralist, but also found in phenomenology and embodied cognition theory (see Chap. 2).
4. This concept will be drawn from both Ian Hacking and Stephen Pinker.
5. The difference in these two ways of bringing about something is that "oughts" or reasons act through agents who (in part) make themselves "as freely acting beings" (Kant (A)3).
6. Gillett (2014a).
7. This is touched on in my 2014b "Mind" paper, but also laid out in *The Discursive Mind* (Harre & Gillett, 1994).
8. This complex view of neural structure emerges from John Hughlings-Jackson's evolutionary neurology (e.g. 1887).
9. The concept is widespread in contemporary neurocognitive theory.

10. The concept was invented by Susan Hurley (2008).
11. The phrase is from Martin Heidegger, but is discussed further in Chap. 4 as a domain of human adaptation.
12. Chemero (2009, p. 85).
13. Chemero (2009, p. 26).
14. Chemero (2009, p. 152), Merleau-Ponty (1962, p. 138). "Getting to grips" has a metaphorical use in relation to the mind, but is deeply resonant with Merleau-Ponty, Wittgenstein, and Heidegger's pragmatist strands.
15. Gillett (1992, 2015).
16. Russell focused on this concept in his work on philosophical logic and the nature of mind (e.g. 1988).
17. JHJ (1887, p. 37).
18. Chemero (2009, p. 152). *The Web of Belief* was a book by WVO Quine and JS Ullian, and it outlined a form of semantic and epistemological holism.
19. Harre and Gillett (1994, 2008) lay out this approach to Kant's community of ends.
20. Such arguments are therefore inadequate to the rich intersubjective encounters wherein language is taught and learnt (Hamlyn, 1973; Merleau-Ponty, 1973; Tomasello, 2014).
21. This is in Lewis Carroll's *Sylvie and Bruno Concluded* (1893).
22. Hurley (1998, p. 34).

## References and Bibliography

Bruner, J. (1990). *Acts of meaning.* Cambridge, MA: Harvard University Press.

Chemero, A. (2009). *Radical embodied cognitive science.* Cambridge, MA: MIT Press.

Cranford, R. (1988). The Persistent Vegetative State: The medical reality (getting the facts straight). *The Hastings Center Report, 18*(1), 27–28.

Damasio, A. (1996). The somatic marker hypothesis and the possible functions of the prefrontal cortex. *Philosophical Transactions of the Royal Society of London, 351,* 1413–1429.

Dennett, D. (1991). *Consciousness explained.* London: Penguin.

Dreyfus, H. L. (2014). *Skillful coping* (M. Wrathall, Ed.). Oxford: Oxford University Press.

Evans, G. (1982). *The varieties of reference.* Oxford: Clarendon.

Freeman, W. (1994). Neural networks and chaos. *Journal of Theoretical Biology, 171,* 13–18.

Freeman, W. (2000). A neurobiological interpretation of semiotics: Meaning, representation and intention. *Information Sciences, 124,* 93–102.

Frege, G. (1977). *Logical investigations* (P. Geach, Trans. & Ed.) Oxford: Blackwell.

Friston, K. (2010). The free energy principle: A unified brain theory? *Nature Reviews/Neuroscience, 11*, 127–134.

Gillett, G. (1992). *Representation, meaning and thought.* Oxford: Clarendon.

Gillett, G. (2014a). Review of Robert Kirk "The conceptual link from mental to physical". *Philosophy, 89*, 352–357. https://doi.org/10.1017/S0031819113000636

Gillett, G. (2014b). Concepts, consciousness and counting by pigeons. *Mind, 123*, 1147–1153.

Gillett, G. (2015). Culture, truth, and science after Lacan. *Journal of Bioethical Inquiry, 12*, 633–644.

Hamlyn, D. (1973). Human learning. In R. Peters (Ed.), *The philosophy of education* (pp. 178–194). Oxford: Oxford University Press.

Harre, R., & Gillett, G. (1994). *The discursive mind.* London: Sage.

Hughlings Jackson, J. (1887). Remarks on the evolution and dissolution of the nervous system. *British Journal of Psychiatry, 33*, 25–48.

Hurley, S. (1998). *Consciousness in action.* Cambridge, MA: Harvard University Press.

Hurley, S. (2008). The shared circuits model (SCM): How control, mirroring, and simulation can enable imitation, deliberation and mindreading. *Behavioral and Brain Sciences, 31*, 1–58.

Levy, N. (2014). *Consciousness and moral responsibility.* Oxford: Oxford University Press.

McDowell, J. (1998). *Mind, value and reality.* Cambridge, MA: Harvard University Press.

Merleau-Ponty, M. (1962). *The phenomenology of perception* (C. Smith, Trans.). London: Routledge.

Merleau-Ponty, M. (1973). *Consciousness and the acquisition of language* (H. Silverman, Trans.). Chicago: Northwestern University Press.

Russell, B. (1988). *On the nature of acquaintance* (pp. 125–174) (reprinted in *Logic and knowledge*). London: Unwin.

Sellars, W. (1997). *Empiricism and the philosophy of mind.* Cambridge, MA: Harvard University Press.

Tomasello, M. (2014). *The natural history of human thinking.* Cambridge, MA: Harvard University Press.

# CHAPTER 2

# From Aristotle to Consciousness and Intentionality

**Abstract** Neo-Aristotelian accounts of the human *psyche* incorporate our meaningful contact with the world such that complex connectivity within the brain and between brain and world is the basis of consciousness and mental function (a "contact view"). Intelligent contact with things shapes human consciousness and cognition in ways reflecting truth-related thought and talk about the world in a context of communication, judgement, and knowledge. Human intersubjectivity thus allows us to triangulate on the objects we encounter and configure our dealings with them in communicable ways grounded in truth and falsity. Aristotle's naturalistic view of the soul as an active, self-organising system implies that distinctively human life corresponds to a progressive integration of neural functions, enabling us to tell (in both senses) what is happening and what things really are.

**Keywords** Autopoiesis • Embodiment • Neurophilosophy • Discursive psychology

> *I knew that seclusion and solitude were very necessary for my friend in those hours of intense mental concentration during which he weighed every particle of evidence, constructed alternative theories, balanced one against the other, and made up his mind as to which points were essential and which immaterial. (p. 205)*

© The Author(s) 2018                                    11
G. Gillett, *From Aristotle to Cognitive Neuroscience*,
https://doi.org/10.1007/978-3-319-93635-2_2

Autopoiesis or self-formation requires insight and self-control. Sherlock Holmes developed the powers of his active mind to the point where he could look to many sources of information, including observations and experiments on diverse topics and everyday substances such as tobacco types and the various kinds of mud in the regions he frequented. Objects and events he encountered contributed to his quite idiosyncratic cognitive profile and its intense and interconnected cognitive maps circuits and their connections to include more and more complex information. When a problem absorbed him, heart and soul, that was reflected in his bodily energy and intense mental focus. John Hughlings-Jackson (JHJ) bridges from brain to mind using the integrative powers that re-adjust neural substrates and adapt the whole organism to its environment, an orientation that sits nicely with Aristotle's two dicta underpinning his naturalistic analysis of the psyche:

1. The soul is in a sense, its objects; and
2. the soul is to the body as sight to the eye.

Neo-Aristotelian accounts of the human *psyche*, as in contemporary phenomenology, put intentionality (or meaning-informed contact with the world in which we live and move and have our being) at the heart of the intellect. That implies that complex connectivity within the brain and between brain and world is the basis of consciousness and mental function ("the contact view"). As we deal (or have intelligent contact) with things, within our thought and talk so as to shape our cognitive selves. For instance, living in a contemporary developed society one learns that small plastic cards afford access to goods and services so that one's opportunities are not determined by the currency one carries. This knowledge reflects cultural practices that structure our subjective engagement with the world. Human cognition uses concepts created in the social, interpersonal, and linguistic contexts constituting culture to give us a multi-faceted grip on the world evident in perception, thought, and action. Thus a city dweller knows to look out for automatic tellers (holes in the wall, banking machines) but the relevant appearances may not be remarkable otherwise. The urban discourse brings forth cards, electronic transactions, and available balances and locates them in our shared practices and ways of reasoning (e.g. "there is not enough in the account to buy that; I must top up.").[1]

Reasoned action and cooperation require human beings to converge in their thought and talk about a series of "third things" in a context of communication, judgement, and knowledge.[2] Triangulation in those terms[3] appears in phenomenology as intersubjectivity and (in developmental psychology) as the relation between thought and language (Vygotsky and Luria). Wittgenstein and Evans adduce insights about semantic rules and the philosophy of thought that, when pursued, lead to a focus on the training that shapes human adaptation and cognitive development. But Aristotle realised that these facets of human natural history create skills of judgement widely employed in our dealings with things and with each other and turn potential into actual thinking.[4]

A similar cognitive-developmental focus is pursued by Merleau-Ponty, who connects human thought, embodiment, language, and intentionality to consciousness:

> The true Cogito does not define the subject's existence in terms of the thought he has of existing, and furthermore does not convert the indubitability of the world into indubitability of thought about the world, nor finally does it replace the world itself by the world as meaning. On the contrary it recognizes my thought itself as an inalienable fact, and does away with any kind of idealism in revealing me as "being-in-the-world". (1962, p. xiv)

Bodily contact with things articulated by shared, sensitive, and skilful techniques informed by semantic content (or meaning) organise perceptuo-motor activity and sustain us in a world that can expose our fragility ("Watch out, that is stinging nettle."). Human cognition is not a calculus fit only for manipulating abstract formulae, but is enmeshed with what we do in the world and how it affects us (the *tuche* or *touch of the world and our dealings with it*). Wittgenstein quotes Goethe to "hit the nail on the head": *In Amfang war die Tat.*[5]

Aristotle's naturalistic and embodied view of the soul as the active principle forming and articulating a distinctively human life[6] embeds a (debated) distinction between the passive and the active intellect. The former indicates our function as a causal system affected by the world and the latter our role as active self-organising, rational, living souls. Our dispositions are shaped by the contingencies acting on us, but, in integrating our neural function, we actively exercise our capacities and learn to tell (both senses) what is happening to us. That enables us to discuss our dealings with things so that mind "work" is "a sort of positive state like light; for in a sense light makes potential colours into actual colours just as we express and work on dispositions that have been formed in us." "Mind, in this sense, is … in its essential nature activity (for always the active is superior to the passive factor, the originating force to the matter which it forms)."[7] Here the active use of the intellect to organise cognitive processes engenders distinctive rational and social skills, producing modes of information use co-created through cooperation and communication to generate knowledge of a shared objective domain of embodied activity. This "enactive theory of consciousness," whereby the dialogues we participate in influence the top-down integration of neural processing, theorises a distinctly human way of fitting our sensori-motor capacities for their highest adaptive context—an interpersonal world.[8] Such a reconfiguration of bodily activity uses propositional abilities and provides a basis for the neuroscientific "binding" of stimuli that belong together as we label manifolds about identified "third things" by constructing perceptuo-motor schemata (served by integrated neural assemblies) (Neisser, 1976) with the help of words. Thus Wittgenstein discusses "seeing-as" in terms of a set of techniques (PI, 208e) that engage a human being with situations (the semantic "gap" between thought and reality creates the possibility of a thought being false or negative (DA[9]; PI #95) in a way that unmediated contact cannot be). Cognition and consciousness therefore rest on multiplex capacities connecting us to a world of contingency within an ethological or discursive domain of communication, meaning, sense-making, and reasoning (Gillett, 2008). Aristotle's active intellect, inter alia, bridges that gap and makes the right connections through what we call judgement—a cognitive skill that must be learnt and practised to give us a grip on the world (Kant, CPR, B174ff). But how do we go from Aristotle to a view of the soul that finesses Cartesian dualism? Franz Brentano, "arguably the most notable bridge figure between the traditions of analytic and continental philosophy" (Jacquette, 6), picks up an embodied enactive view of the mind from Aristotle's naturalism and inspires the phenomenology of Merleau-Ponty in a way that parallels embodied cognition theory (Gallagher, 2005). But whereas both Merleau-Ponty and Brentano come to terms with the content and structure of human thought as they appear in philosophical logic, embodied cognition theory struggles in reconciling natural purposes and biological adaptation with philosophical logic. Brentano argued that "objective scientific philosophical psychology takes priority over all other branches of philosophy" and adopted "reism"—an ontology of actual existents—rather than representationalism—an ontology of internal representations of the world into his account of intentionality (Jacquette, 2004, p. 7). Conceptual analysis, combined with scientific discovery (Jacquette, 2004, p. 18), renders intentionality in terms of relations to objects seen in some specific way. In that sense, they *inexist* the mental acts in which they appear. This is not—as is often thought—a form of representationalism that contradicts reism (an ontology of real things in a real world), but rather it follows Aristotle by noting that imagination (and possible falsity) extend and characterise the ways we think of things so that we need recourse to reason and argument to disentangle truth and falsity. Wittgenstein affirms both our contact with the world and the semantic gap when he remarks:

> [W]e—and our meaning—do not stop anywhere short of the fact; but ... *Thought* can be of what is *not* the case. (PI, #95)

We are left wondering how consciousness emerges from embodiment, first nature, and the "space of reasons" created by communication and argument. A well-crafted account of that emergence undermines causal or functional theories of representation as supervenient and dependent on internal neural processes (in terms of both content and realisation) and reminds philosophy of its proper role.[10] In part this emerges when we pursue the remarks already noted.

# 1   ARISTOTLE, EMBODIED HUMAN LIFE, AND SECOND NATURE

## 1.1   Embodiment

To trace the natural growth of the human soul, the basis of consciousness and cognition as part of a human life, we can begin with Aristotle's claim that a living soul—our form as subjective beings—is embodied:

> [W]e can wholly dismiss as unnecessary the question whether the soul and the body are one: it is as meaningless as to ask whether the wax and the shape given to it by the stamp are one, or generally the matter of a thing and that of which it is the matter. Unity has many senses (as many as 'is' has), but the most proper and fundamental sense ... is the relation of an actuality to that of which it is the actuality. ... Suppose that the eye were an animal— sight would have been its soul, for sight is the substance or essence of the eye ... the eye being merely the matter of seeing; when seeing is removed the eye is no longer an eye, except in name—it is no more a real eye than the

eye of a statue or of a painted figure. We must now extend our consideration from the 'parts' to the whole living body; for what the departmental sense is to the bodily part which is its organ, that the whole faculty of sense is to the whole sensitive body as such. [DA, 412b 5–23]

The crux of tembodiment, as a human soul is the nervous system and its evolution as can be seen by unpacking Aristotle's two remarks above: (i) "the soul is in a sense, its objects" (DA, 431b21); and (ii) "the soul is to the body as sight to the eye" (DA, 412b21). Consider sight, the eye, and colour perception: perceiving that X *is red* links vision and discourse in that when a thinker says, "That is red," s/he exercises a complex skill that constitutes a grasp of the concept *red*. It rests on discerning the colour when perceiving something red (as distinct from the texture or level of illumination) but also on realising that the colour is, in English, called "red," making the judgement required. Thus:

> How do I know that is red?—It would be an answer to say, "I have learnt English." (PI, #381)

A perceptual judgement *that is red* therefore embeds a set of "grammatical" rules governing the mental ascriptions inherent in colour perception and the requisite (visual and communicative) skills that enable intelligent visual engagement in the relevant situations where language is taught and learnt (Gillett, 1992, p. 77ff). One learns to be an accurate perceiver (who can tell what s/he is looking at) in that learning process. Our perceptuo-motor skills are thereby linked with discourse so that we are able to tell (in both senses) how things are. That perceptual thinking is therefore, as Kant observed, discursive and shaped in an objective-reflective-normative (ORN) domain of human communication (Tomasello, 1999, p. 123) and is related to (the aptly named) "semantic memory" (Neisser, 1982, pp. 79–86). This kind of neurocognitive development is inherently autopoietic or self-making, a capacity of the *active intellect*, as in a tendentious interpretation of *De Anima*.

Several key points emerge from this wax and its imposed form analogy that converge with embodied cognition theory and enactivism:

1. Aristotle affirms a basic ontology of form and matter jointly constituting a substance so that in any actual thing both aspects are inseparable (Sorabji, 1974);

2. he notices that the unity of the soul is compatible with logical distin-guishability—a philosophical device used in analysis, not an actual separation or decomposition into parts to highlight the fact that the matter of the wax is suited to be a vehicle of its form (as a seal) but does not produce that form
3. which is linked to integrated natural functioning not just physical or material mechanisms; *and*
4. he analyses integrated function as a feature of the whole living (we can add, *evolved*) body.

Within the integrated whole, the "higher" powers of the soul, such as those of the intellect, themselves form a holistic evolved set of functions operating together:

> [A]ll animals that possess the sense of touch have also appetition. The case of imagination is obscure; we must examine it later. Certain kinds of animals possess in addition the power of locomotion, and still another order of ani-mate beings, i.e. man and possibly another order like man or superior to him, the power of thinking, i.e. mind. [DA 414b 12–16]

Aristotle relates thinking to an hierarchy of function built on a base of appetite and movement—the free-ranging pursuit of organismic interests or affordances,[11] a term that relates cognition to opportunities and threats in the environment and meshes closely with Wittgenstein's account of thought: "concepts lead us to make investigations; are the expression of our interest, and direct our interest" (PI, #570). Ecological, enactivist, embodied views of this type link perception and action to an interested sensori-motor "coupling" with the environment, recalling the "inten-tional arc" (which also has symbolic aspects) and the way we are con-nected to (or get a grip on) a world of action.[12] Subjectivity and consciousness are grounded by the intentional arc in action and embodi-ment (Hurley, 1998) such that the hierarchy in cognitive evolution culmi-nates in a triad of intellectual capacities—calculation, imagination, and thinking:

> What is the soul of plant, animal, man? ... the facts are that the power of perception is never found apart from the power of self-nutrition, while—in plants—the latter is found isolated from the former. Again, no sense is found apart from that of touch, while touch is found by itself; many animals have

neither sight, hearing, nor smell. Again, among living things that possess sense some have the power of locomotion, some not. Lastly, certain living beings—a small minority—possess calculation and thought, for (among mortal beings) those which possess calculation have all the other powers above ... while the converse does not hold—indeed some live by imagination alone, while others have not even imagination. The mind that knows with immediate intuition presents a different problem. [DA 414b30–415a11]

Calculation is here contrasted to imagination and linked to thought and both are distinguished from the intuitive (coupled and holistic) mind. This text must be handled carefully, but it implies that coupled activity provoked by actual encounters with objects or situations has effects "long after the removal of the instigating stimulus" and yet "yields sensory-like consequences" (Robinson, 1989, p. 68). These lingering cognitive connections cause a creature to react "as if its contents were real" and are, therefore, possibly misleading (p. 69). Reason elaborates and refines impressions so that imagination forms part of an integrated system of anticipation and response generated from past experience and moderated by argument. Thought, in blending imagination and calculation, incorporates argument-refining mental contents in ways that are communicable and sustainable under reflection (so that, as in Kant, thinking is a discursive activity [CPR, B93]).[13] In that way the intellectual powers of the soul grow and develop;

> [I]f we are to express .... what the thinking power is, or the perceptive, or the nutritive, we must ... first give an account of thinking or perceiving, for in the order of investigation the question of what an agent does precedes the question, what enables it to do what it does. If this is correct, we must on the same ground go yet another step farther back and have some clear view of the objects of each; thus we must start with these objects, e.g. with food, with what is perceptible, or with what is intelligible. [DA 415a 20–25]

Embodied cognition within such an ecological account captures the dynamic relation between subject and world, thereby countering both idealism and internalist representationalism (Adams, Drebushenko, Fuller, & Stecker, 1990) and endorsing a "contact" form of realism (Dreyfus & Taylor, 2015).

Aristotle continues, further analysing the powers of the human soul: (1) local movement and (2) thinking, discriminating, and perceiving:

Thinking, both speculative and practical, is akin to a form of perceiving; for in the one as well as the other the soul discriminates and is cognizant of something which is. [DA, 427a 25–26]

"Something which is," if "like is known as/perceived by/acted upon by like," implies that thinker and object of thought coexist, interact with, and affect each other (the "coupled oscillation" of embodied cognition theory or Aristotle's immediacy of our "perception of special objects"). Error and intentional selectivity (as distinct from such "oscillation" or perceptuo-motor holism) are possible when a shadow falls between consciousness and intentionality and contact with the real world arising from the complex of thought, imagination, and reasoning (Caston, 1996); "it is a received principle that error as well as knowledge in respect to contraries is one and the same" [DA, 427b 5–6]. One could say thought and reason arise in response to the possibility of negation (to echo Frege—"a thought" something for which the question of truth can arise[14]—and Wittgenstein's "thought can be of what is not the case").

The contact view, interpreted in the light of Wittgenstein's remark that thought and meaning "do not stop anywhere short of the fact" and yet thought can be of what is not the case (PI #95), recalls the predictive brain whereby a thinker constantly formulates what might be encountered in terms prepared to inform action.[15] Sartre's pregnant observation that I can perceive that Pierre is not in the Café points us towards the mind producing anticipations or expectations out of prior experience, betraying an interested concern about the world and my being in it (Heidegger's *sorge*). That orientation is crucial to an embodied subject, whereas purely abstract and disembodied thought or logic intends nothing because it is not interested and has no reason to care. Human thought, by contrast, is jointly grounded in our appetitive relation to a world of contingency and our normative relation to truth because error in thought and action is of vital significance to us. Aristotle again:

Further, speculative thinking is also distinct from perceiving—I mean that in which we find rightness and wrongness—rightness in prudence, knowledge, true opinion, wrongness in their opposites; for perception of the special objects of sense is always free from error, and is found in all animals, while it is possible to think falsely as well as truly, ... thought is found only where there is discourse of reason as well as sensibility. For imagination is different from either perceiving or discursive thinking, though it is not found without sensation, or judgement without it. ... this activity is not the same kind of thinking as judgement ... For imagining lies within our own power whenever we wish (e.g. we can call up a picture, as in the practice of mnemonics by the use of mental images), but in forming opinions we cannot escape the alternative of falsehood or truth. Further, when we think something to be fearful or threatening, emotion is immediately produced, and so too with what is encouraging; but when we merely imagine we remain as unaffected as persons who are looking at a painting of some dreadful or encouraging scene. [DA, 427b 13–28]

Aristotle's discussion touches on a series of topics important for embodied enactivism: (i) the special objects of sense and their relation to objects, (ii) the *normative relation* between thought and truth, (iii) the *discursive character* of thought, (iv) the role of *judgement* in keeping touch with reality, and (v) the *affordances* central to engaged rather than speculative (or "offline") thinking. All of these are relevant to the way that human beings grow/make the evolved nervous system into the biological basis of the human soul:

1. The *senses and their proper targets* (coupling) are found in all animals and underpin cognitive engagement. Sensori-motor coupling is not thought and yet consciousness is constantly and variably thoughtful and open to rationally constrained reflection.
2. *Normativity:* note that this is regulative (Kant) or ideal (Husserl), but that cognitive abilities, once mastered in developing second nature through discipline and training, can actively be employed otherwise than in contact with the world—counterfactually, deceptively, in simulation, pretence or rhetoric, poetically, metaphorically, and other forms of offline cognitive work.
3. *Discourse*, where truth and falsity are at stake, engenders argument, the crucible of second nature, where right thinking about the actual (shared and publically accessible) world is negotiated and refined through discursive interactions rather than through the (potentially mortal) trial and error of the "tooth and claw" function.
4. *Judgement*, as Kant noted (CPR, B171ff), is a set of skills that are trained in relation to a public domain of objects or examples in which we triangulate and to which we apply powers of abstraction in the service of selective representation and reasoning (A, 14).

5. *Affordances*: when "the rubber hits the road," thought must get a grip so that it is effectively linked to a domain of adaptation inhabited by the thinker (a being-in-the-world-with-others); that is, where anticipation is useful and action becomes effective.

Aristotle summarises his thoughts in various ways but in each the soul is an animating, integrative principle of life engaging thinker and world through concept use and rational or discursive refinement; the soul is, on that analysis, not a reified immaterial (Cartesian dualist) or rationalist but material (Cartesian internalist/physicalist) entity observing human life as lived but the actual creature fitted for a distinctively human form of life:

> The soul is the cause or source of the living body. The terms cause and source have many senses. But the soul is the cause of its body in ... three senses ... It is (a) the source or origin of movement, it is (b) the end, it is (c) the essence of the whole living body in relation to which there are no separable parts despite the conceptual distinctions which can be applied. (DA, 213b 30–37)

The inseparable combination of active and passive aspects of the intellect in *De Anima* comprises second nature so that these "parts of soul ... are, in spite of certain statements to the contrary, incapable of separate existence though ... distinguishable by definition" or, as also translated, "conceptually distinct" [413b, 27–30].[16] The analysis reveals "perception as a constructive, and not merely a receptive faculty" (Robinson, 1989, p. 66) so that the active intellect is "the power which enables ... knowledge to be abstracted" (Rist, 1966, p. 11). Embodied cognition theories often focus on coupled sensori-motor oscillators, but Kant's "spontaneity and receptivity" (often interpreted within a representationalist rather than a contact framework) focuses on Aristotle's active/passive distinction to look at our making of ourselves as freely acting beings (A, 3). Both Rist and Haldane (1992) distance Aristotle's doctrine of the active and passive intellect from Platonic or dualistic interpretations of them as parts of a soul metaphysically separate from the natural world. The idea of complex, integrated neurocognitive assemblies triply responsive (to the embodied subject, actual world targets, and discourse) frames *the soul* as a conceptual "take" on our natural being-in-the-world and thereby "a contribution to the understanding of nature" and our "innate and acquired modes of adaptation" (Robinson, 1989, p. 50).

Aristotle's active intellect affirms that a human being as a whole (integrated) being is active in thinking [DA, 417a-b] and not just a system of structured states in functional relations acting when triggered to do so in ways that exhibit a formalisable syntax and system of causal transitions—the underlying framework of functionalism (Kim, 2010):

> [H]e can in the absence of any external counteracting cause realize his knowledge in actual knowing at will. This implies a third meaning of "a knower" (c), one who is already realizing his knowledge—he is a knower in actuality and in the most proper sense is knowing, e.g. this A. Both the former are potential knowers, who realize their respective potentialities, the one (a) by change of quality, i.e. repeated transitions from one state to its opposite under instruction, the other (b) by the transition from the inactive possession of sense or grammar to their active exercise. [DA, 417a25–b1]

Active thinking, we could say, is more than being set up for certain cognitive transitions and the skills used therein are dynamic reciprocal and resonant, giving perception a complex (for Aristotle, tripartite) quality: (1) we are immediately acquainted with an object of sensation (the thing that catches our attention); (2) we detect and track certain qualities "concomitant" in it—or, using the voice of some neuroscientists, we could say, "we bind certain elements of the sensory manifold together" (the green moving thing, or the red figure bounded on three sides) by picking up or abstracting certain affordance-related facets of the object; and (3) we characterise the object according to discursively based categories or universals (such as *frog*, *triangle*, etc.). This analysis underpins a dissection of error in perception [DA, 428b]:

> The motion which is due to the activity of sense in these three modes of its exercise will differ from the activity of sense; (1) the first kind of derived motion is free from error while the sensation is present; (2) and (3) the others may be erroneous whether it is present or absent, especially when the object of perception is far off. If the imagination presents no other features than those enumerated and is what we have described, then imagination must be a movement resulting from an actual exercise of a power of sense [429a].

Aristotle's analysis plausibly informs Kant's account of imagination (CPR, B179–181) and converges with the neuroscience of imaging and imagination (Bartolomeo, 2002). The active intellect, to use a term from embodied cognition theory, "brings forth" an object for thought from the oscillatory coupling between the active sensori-motor subject and a context:

> Since in every class of things, as in nature as a whole, we find two factors involved, (1) a matter which is potentially all the particulars included in the class, (2) a cause which is productive in the sense that it makes them all (the latter standing to the former, as e.g. an art to its material), these distinct elements must likewise be found within the soul. ... where the alternative of true or false applies, there we always find a putting together of objects of thought in a quasi-unity. [DA, 430a 24–26]

*Poiesis* or productive putting together (*nous poetikos*) of the sensory input here prefigures Kant's *synthesis* (possibly through the lens of Thomas Aquinas [Haldane, 1992]). Our knowledge of objects is seen as resting on perceptuo-motor cycles and cognitive schemata (Neisser, 1976) integrated by the top-down effects of semantic connections in a discursive arena where we pursue our appetites or interests (as in enactive theories of consciousness) and learn to tell what is going on:

> The faculty of thinking then thinks the forms in the images, and ... what is to be pursued or avoided is marked out for it, so where there is no sensation and it is engaged upon the images it is moved to pursuit or avoidance. [DA, 431b 4–6]

In this passage Aristotle gives an account of the motive/emotive effects of imagination and our agency in those mental acts in which states of the soul (or a neurocognitive system) are sorted into potential—or structural—and those which are active:

> [T]he expression "to be acted upon" has more than one meaning; it may mean either (a) the extinction of one of two contraries by the other, or (b) the maintenance of what is potential by the agency of what is actual and already ... acted upon, ... one's being actual and the other potential. [DA, 417b]

Here we see our grasp of a cognitive (or grammatical)[17] structure translated into an active strand of thought that prevails against alternatives (Haldane, 1992, p. 207) as the agent, through "acts and inner determinations" (CPR, B574), conceptualises a situation in a certain way.

Conceptualising (or rendering in semantic form) is constrained by the couplings underpinning it but influenced or inflected by sediments or residues of previous encounters and arguments so that intentional states, like bodily habits, have a history.[18] A mental act thereby enacts a potential state, prefigured in the agent by previous experience and argument; it does so by responding to and focusing on actual and possible contingencies in the current situation. These are conceptually enabled by and based on communication, reasoning, and argument, a line of thought that resonates with Brentano's link between consciousness and intentionality (Gillett & McMillan, 2001). Such an analysis blocks dualist views of intentional inexistence or immanent intentionality—interpreted as entities indwelling the mind (Jacquette, 2004, p. 7). Perception, tied to objects and elaborated by the active intellect, implies Brentano's later "re-ist" metaphysics focusing on real particulars encountered in experience (Jacquette, 2004, p. 10), and extended by argument so (e.g.) *the green dragon outside my window* is a construct from traces left by being in contact with actual things supplemented by discursive posits.

## 1.2    Second Nature and Skills Mobilised in Cognition

That certain behaviour is second nature to someone implies that it is habitual or characteristic for them to act or think in a certain way and that doing what they do seems natural to them. McDowell notes: "the practical intellect's coming to be as it ought to be is the acquisition of second nature, involving the moulding of motivational and evaluative propensities: a process that takes place in nature,"[19] but not merely biological nature: "the dictates of virtue have acquired an authority abdicated by first nature with the onset of reason."[20] He goes on to argue that when we question what we do and ask if we should do this or that, nature's dictates become negotiable (thus, for Hughlings-Jackson, conscious acts are the least automatic because many sources of information affect the causal pathways). Aristotle regards developed, intentional ways of acting as shaped by reason, argument, and self-adaptation trained in human ways of being and the rules governing thought and our mutual assessments of one another. The shaping of the intellect by reason and argument means that human second nature is jointly determined by intersubjectivity and natural contingency,[21] a process whereby culture engenders practices that inject meaning into an extensional ("disenchanted") or purely contingent world.[22]

McDowell notes that second nature is not explicit in Aristotle so that his own exposition of it largely concerns virtue and brings into view many constitutive features of the human soul that seem familiar and natural and build on what biology endows to us. Aristotle regards virtue as modifying our contact with our world through practices of self-formation that allow us to moderate and even act contrary to what animal nature urges.[23] In a similar way, Merleau-Ponty regards sedimentation from experience (contact) and modification by language as the means whereby we pass

> from a quasi-biological activity to one that is nonbiological ... a whole movement, or activity, that has integrated it into a dialogue.
> The child's receives the "sense" of language from his environment.
> The word arrives as a summary and pruning down of a larger unformulated richness of experience.
> The appearance of the first words suddenly makes the relationship of *the sign to the signified* explicit.
> Language is attained not as an articulatory phenomenon but as an element in a linguistic game.
> The child's movement toward speech is a constant appeal to others.[24]

The intersubjectivity of Merleau-Ponty's analysis gestures at a phenomenological route to a view rich enough to relate second nature to the human soul in terms accessible to contemporary philosophy of mind and moral philosophy.

## 2   BRENTANO, SECOND NATURE, AND THE CONTENTS OF CONSCIOUSNESS

Brentano's "psychognosy" (conceptual psychology) pursues Aristotle's naturalism alongside the logical structure of experience to lay the foundations for a "science of consciousness." He anticipates the current neuroscience of perception by identifying three logical moments of a perceptual act. Electrocorticographic (ECoG) records of the response to visual stimuli, in fact, reveal waves of excitation remarkably convergent with Brentano's (1874 [1973], 1929 [1981]) account to reveal three phases of selective attention:

1. detecting the object (or targeting, noticing);

2. distinguishing it from its context (binding its stimulus characteristics); and

3. comparing it with others (categorising it, attaching a semantic marker to it).

These "moments" coincide in "the blink of an eye," yielding "clear and distinct ideas" of perceived objects:

1. The first moment corresponds to the subject's attention being caught by something, manifest in speech as, for instance, "What's that?" This immediate or primary visual phase reflects the brain registering the stimulus as something to be attended to and interconnected within a global cognitive workspace (Baars, 2002; Dehaene & Naccache, 2001).

2. The second moment—differentiation—or, in neuroscience, "binding" (Treisman, 1996) indicates the genesis of a dynamic predictive "model"—a quasi-stable associational complex apt for comparison with extant global attractors (patterns of excitation which, through familiarity, are favoured) in the neural network (Friston, 2010). It goes beyond noticing and creates an action-oriented pattern of neural firing in the organism's workspace. Phases of disorder or chaos (Friston's "free energy") in the brain show associations that are inconclusive or unresolved, but they energise new potential channels of cognition or control of behaviour. Resolutions of these chaotic moments capture Gestalt distinctions between figure and ground whereby a perceiver actively distinguishes those elements constituting the object as something to be thought about in a particular way (e.g. as a duck not a rabbit). Such resolutions enact the effects of learning on weighted symbolic information in the brain (King et al., 2013) and link the current stimulus array to a response repertoire and a "third moment" of perception—comparison.

3. The third moment "slots" a stimulus array into a subject's cognitive/pragmatic lexicon by classifying it as indicating an object of a certain kind. Brentano uses various terms (some drawn from Kant): comparison, subsumption under a general concept (different sensory presentations are cognitively unified to potentiate a response), differentiation (from other objects and other types of object), or clarifying analysis (1929, p. 13), arguing that this may be a quasi-mathematical process (1929, p. 9) whereby simultaneous and multiple positive and nega-

tive connections evident in current neural activity link the present manifold of information to patterns already captured by the system (a Bayesian process responsive to top-down effects from discursive regularities). Kant speaks of "abstraction," a power of the mind which compares and contrasts representations and applies certain categories that potentiate judgements and action (CPR, B130); A, 14–15. He thereby indicates what is actively being done to the configuration of a cognitive system as the soul adapts itself through learning.

Taken together, the three moments of perception/experience reveal an autopoietic process that can be variously described: the interactive cycle of perception to generate schemata (Neisser), Gestalt differentiation of figure from ground, the binding of stimulus properties within an action-related representation, and so on. These are neurophilosophical characterisations of the way that the soul elaborates its structures of sensori-motor engagement (or contact):

> The person who differentiates compares; and the person who compares notices the two things that he compares. ... the object of an act of sensing very often encompasses a great diversity. The act of sensing relates to a whole in its totality, but, of course, refers to the parts as well, yet only in so far as they are given explicitly with the object; it does not explicitly stand in a particular relation to each individual part. (Brentano, 1929, p. 21)

Contacts between embodied perceivers and objects generate global attractors in the predictive brain (Friston) and top-down confluences of weighted mutual symbolic information (wMSI) link together multiple areas of excitation to create neural assemblies connected with discursive activity. An intentional relationship to an object creates mental phenomena and grounds a multiplex process in which emotion, reason, action, and memory (Hughlings-Jackson, 1887) are integrated to form global attractor states as part of a predictive model of the world apt for action or cognition. Thus, when I notice the fly on the wall, I inevitably notice it *as something meaningful* (e.g. a black speck, a piece of dirt, or a fly), so that the relevant content specifications are linked both to a state of the world (the *referent* in a Fregean scheme of sense and reference) and to a way of thinking and talking about it (the analogue of sense [*Sinn*] or cognitive significance [Frege, 1980; Husserl, 1982, p. 307ff]). Therefore cognitive or cerebral connectivity is explicated by noticing how I differentiate the object from context or ground and engage it with structures of meaning in ways I am moved to by my interests. The resulting triply responsive cognitive activity (responding to the world, self, and discourse) underpins phenomenological accounts whereby human subjectivity creates a world of intentionality and cooperative purposes built on contact.

The third (discursive) arm of our response is discursive because human beings use sense (*Sinn*) to inform consciousness and share knowledge through symbol use or language (Luria, 1973). All animals direct their sensori-motor activity in relation to things around them and, in that sense, share a basic aspect of consciousness with us, but beyond animal flexibility and integration of attention and behaviour (to salient objects and also to significant aspects of their environment), human beings use language to develop and master shared techniques of selective attention, differentiation, and articulation of experience within a multi-perspectival and normative context (of rules). The relevant norms (implicit in rule-following) sustain a range of cognitive adaptations enabling novice thinkers to organise their activity by "ratcheting it up" using mutuality and intersubjectivity (Merleau-Ponty, Tomasello, Pinker, Sperber, Gillett) and creating a distinctly human "second nature."

The active elaboration of contact within a connected workspace based on patterns of coherence between different cortical and subcortical circuits in the brain (Freeman, 2015) evident in ECoG data is the neurophilosophical "triple beat" of cognition:

1. reception of a pattern of excitation in a localised cerebral area (e.g. the visual cortex);
2. a give-and-return communication with closely associated areas that add detail to the stimulus as an object is apprehended multi-modally (e.g. visual, auditory, proprioceptive, and spatial senses); and
3. an evaluation of the apprehended object in relation to affordances or adaptively relevant opportunities processed by widespread areas of the brain, critically mediated—triply indirectly—by the ventromedial prefrontal cortex (Damasio, 1996).

The latencies between the received signal and these two subsequent phases of processing reflect cerebral proximity and complexity of connectivity so that progressive timing delays are the inverse of bandwidths of cerebral activity (3 Hz, 14 Hz, 20 Hz, etc.) and implicitly validate the Aristotelian and phenomenological analyses (Freeman, 2015; Kosma, Davies, & Freeman, 2012).

## 3    KANT AND HUSSERL: INTENTIONALITY
## AND ANTHROPOLOGY

Kant and Husserl further our understanding of intentionality as the key to second nature, the human *psyche* and human thought. Both give neo-Aristotelian accounts of the active nature of cognition, as human adaptation inflects contact by a normative framework of reason (conveyed by instruction and argument). Thus we have a triple process in which predictive cognitive modelling is inflected by the top-down effect of social, interpersonal, and discursive activity on our neural processing of our contact with the world.

### 3.1    *Kant: The Anthropology of Second Nature*

Kant's spontaneity (B132)—invokes the active and pragmatic aspects of mind and consciousness. His term *gemut*—the pragmatic and moral self as distinct from *seele*—self as I appear to myself through inner sense (CPR, B37, B158), draws attention to the active generation of action and thought. The human soul, informed by sensation and perception (CPR, B74), is embodied: "the mind is by itself alone ... the principle of life ... in union with body" (CJ, 119) but, not fixed by instinct. Rather it is, through second nature, open ended and self-devised through education and social relations.[25]

Foucault, analysing Kant's *Anthropology*, remarks: (A), distinction of *gemut* from *seele* in terms of the active, principled use of intellectual powers to deal with the contingencies of life (FiKA, 60–62) by contrast with complex inner states imperfectly known. The active intellect engages in "synthesis," abstraction, and action, making sense of experience in terms that reflect reason and understanding (CPR, B130). A human soul, through "acts and inner determinations," makes something of itself and its contacts (A, 3) that is manifest when human cognition is deployed to serve natural purposes (CJ, 217). *Seele* (the self of introspection as we observe our own cognising) is often poorly understood as a domain of infallible processes because self-action is not easily separable from self-observation (A, 31). We can therefore make errors about our inner lives because of our fallible empirical or psychological consciousness of ourselves. Determinate or "logical consciousness" of ourselves differs in that we actively exercise selected and learnt cognitive capacities, for example, for *abstraction* to do intellectual work and act intelligently: (i) "abstracting a definition from the object of my sense impressions" (A, 14); and (ii) selectively attending to aspects of a stimulus array or manifold, as in shutting one's eyes to "a wart on a sweetheart's face or to a gap where teeth are missing" (A, 15) shows "freedom of the faculty of thought and sovereignty of the mind" (Gillett & Liu, 2012). That active use of intellect is evident, for instance, in aspect seeing (PI, II.11) and implicit in concept mastery, where we achieve, for instance, "the *unity of the action of bringing various representations under a common one* ... based on the spontaneity of thinking" (CPR, B93). Such cognitive skills are moulded (in Aristotelian fashion) as we are trained in relation to concrete examples (B173) so that we become able to subsume diverse representations and bring forth "objects of thought" (Chemero)[26] from our contact with the world that are apt to be communicated about (A, 14).

*Developing judgement* (an activity of the soul as *gemut*) is, therefore, mastery of a skill the lack of which no formal instruction can make good (CPR B172)—it applies (and is not instructed by) rules:

> General logic contains no precepts at all for the power of judgment and moreover cannot contain them. ... Now if it wanted to show generally how one ought to subsume under those rules, i.e., distinguish whether something stands under them or not, this could not happen except once again through a rule. But just because this is a rule, it would demand another instruction for the power of judgment. (CPR, B172)

Judgement therefore cannot be explicitly taught but only practised and shaped (as in Aristotle) so that the power of judgement is not only "*a natural gift*" (CPR, B172 ), albeit linked to purposive activity, but also an art shaped out of natural function (CJ, #23, 84) by "enaction," "autopoiesis," or self-organisation (Thompson & Varela, 2001, p. 419). Second nature, in short, characterises the human soul as a product shaped out of first/animal nature by education and discursive experience.

### 3.2    Husserl: Consciousness and Intersubjectivity

Husserl builds on Aristotelian strands in Kant in terms picked up by Merleau-Ponty's philosophy of embodied cognition. Thus Husserl's transcendental ego (Zahavi, 2005, p. 14)—whereby one conceives of oneself as oneself—is, as Aristotle noted, a conceptualisation of the active embodied subject as a complex, cognitive, psychosomatic, and social entity in contact with a shared natural world:

It is easy to convince oneself that the material world is not just any portion of the natural world but its fundamental stratum ... [but] It fails to include the souls of animals and men ... together with their conscious relationship to the world surrounding them ... *here consciousness and thinghood form a connected whole.* (*Ideas*[G] 114)

Husserl recognises our intentional being-in-the-world: "an intentional experience is actual, carried out, that is, after the manner of the cogito, the subject directs itself within it towards the intentional object" (*Ideas*[G] 109); "we are directed—not only in an apprehending way—also to the value. Not merely the representing of the matter in question but also the appreciating" (p. 110). Here is integrative enactivity—the work of bringing forth the object, its associated affects, and the horizon against which it appears.

Husserl notes that a single unitary mental act (e.g. of believing, perceiving, loving, etc.) implies a "multiplicity" of *hyle*, *noesis*, and *noema*; the first two *hyle*—experiential matter and *noesis*—a way of knowing, constitute the actual mental activity immanent in the experience, and the latter, the intentional content or norms governing meaning (he uses the terms *reele* and the *Irreelles*, respectively [the latter often translated as ideal]). Thus noesis—intellectual activity or cognitive processing—works on *hyle* (our real-world sensori-motor coupling) and together they yield articulate contents of experience constrained by norms themselves not part of internal cognitive processes (*Ideas*[G], 261ff) but rather normatively related to the noetic content as follows:

1. the *de re* situation, part of the world, with which thinking engages and the site where we track objects perceptuo-cognitively (e.g. following the flight of a bumblebee); and
2. *noemata*—elements of the normative framework by which thought is structured (e.g. the form of a tree), a transcendental domain of rules and logical properties delineating the contents that presentations can be properly judged to instance and drawn from "an intersubjective world ... accessible in respect of its Objects to everyone" (1950, p. 91).

The intersubjective domain of communication and argument is where "we ... have the world pregiven in this 'together' as ... existing for us and to which we, together, belong" (1954, p. 109). Within this domain of mutual action and interaction, "self consciousness and consciousness of others are inseparable" (1954, p. 253). Thus *I* (as thinker) exist as a first-person correlate of *you* and *he*, a being among others who engages with me. In this context we are taught and teach each other the rules that make us capable of well-crafted judgements about the world (CPR, B172ff).

*Noesis*, the result of combining intersubjectively communicated norms—*noemata*—with our worldly engagement, therefore comprises skills incorporating a "multiplicity of validities" (Husserl, 1954, p. 163) such that a naturalistic reading of *Sinn* (or logical sense) emerges: *Sinn* rests on discursive or intersubjective norms inherent in and emergent from communicating about shared actual experience, an insight that eluded Frege (Gillett, 1997).

Husserl's analysis of thought and meaning implies that human souls inhabit the natural world and discursively hone their cognitive skills through training, correction, and argument (CPR, B172). The intellectual powers of the human soul therefore rest on communicability without ambiguity (as Frege insisted). It emerges among intelligent, embodied subjects and their communication about what they do (Gillett, 2008; McDowell, 1998; Sellars, 1997; Tomasello, 1999). Thus second nature is shaped by the complex intellectual, socio-cultural, and pragmatic reality of the human ecosphere.

### 3.3    Human Cognition, Consciousness, and Concepts

These "psychognosic" aspects of cognition have certain features. They meet Evans' "generality constraint" (GC), derived from the predicate calculus (Hurford, 2003) as a theoretical analysis of logic and argument. The GC aims to distinguish mere responding from conscious thought (Evans, 1982, p. 104; Gillett, 2014). It "delineates the flexibility and power of conscious thought over more modular and limited responding". It states that a thinker who is able to frame a thought of the form <a is F>, for example, <*that block is square*>, must employ two abilities, one *referential* and the other *predicative*. The *first* is abstracted from repeated presentations of a given object such as *that block* and enables a subject to think of *that block* as an enduring numerical individual experientially re-identifiable as a potential bearer of a range of predicates in a series of thoughts such as <*that block is yellow*>, <*that block is square*>, <*that block has rolled over*>, <*that block is beside the red one*>, and so on. The *second* ability is predicative—indicated by the term F in *Fa* (e.g. "a is *square*"), and reflects the ability to apply a single predicate to different particulars (as in <*that red* *patch is square>, <that box is square>, <that card is square>,* etc.). A (predicative) ability tracks an identifiable feature of the world designated by a general or property term requiring a thinker to abstract just the feature denoted by the general concept (here, *<square>*). The subject can then link the present array to others on the basis that they share that feature.

The first ability—to pick out and "track" an object as a particular—involves neurocognitively binding the diverse features and temporally dispersed presentations of the object together within a single unified neurocognitive assembly (for Kant, one form of empirical synthesis [B196–197]). The second links different such assemblies. A subject with abilities of these two types is capable of a range of thoughts involving objects and the properties they instance (so as to form communicable truth-related propositions. That creature is therefore responsive to argument about and not just sensori-motor coupling) to a world of objects and properties (Gillett, 1992). What is more, the relevant abilities enable a creature to form a cognitive map of a shared ORN domain rather than merely encoding a set of triggers to react thus and so when certain stimulus patterns appear. A map-forming ability of that type plausibly embeds an organism's understanding of "the antecedent-consequent relations among external events in the absence of its own direct involvement" (Tomasello, 1999, p. 23). Thus the GC implies that human consciousness rests on articulation and dynamic responsiveness that potentiates a rich, flexible, and contestable intentionality (Gillett & McMillan, 2001), enabling the active formation of propositional attitudes, reason-governed action, and dynamic participation in a meaningful domain transcending an individual thinker (Gillett, 2014; Zahavi, 2003).

The link between consciousness, intentionality, and the structure of thought implicates a holistic set of cognitive abilities used by embodied human subjects to make sense of a dynamic stream of experience and track regular and recurring features of an objective world. That sense embeds rules mapping those features onto communicable content with a normative structure (Davidson, 1980). Experience structured in this way potentiates *consciousness of* things as red, square, frogs, warm, moving, and so on. This distinctive richness of human experience reflects developed skills of focused attention and abstraction, trained in a thinker by other thinkers and picking out a potentially infinite variety of aspects of the world that are referred to, communicated about, and reflected upon. Hume's (1740, p. 676) claim that consciousness is a succession of contentful states rather than an empty inner presence—"I" the subject—highlights but then fails to analyse the active work that is going on in human experience which implies second nature is formed within a realm of communication and propositional content grounded on truth and falsity (as Aristotle noted). The active nature of cognition underpins the unity of cognition and consciousness usefully interpreted as broadcasting information within a global workspace (Baars, 2002) comprising interwoven neural assemblies responsive to self, the world, and discourse. This view embraces a conception of the embodied subject who integrates the human "cognitive workspace" (with a little help from his or her friends) so as to bring forth objects of thought, replete with action-related properties and relations.

Active and interactive cognition as the ground on which intentionality or "aboutness" is an essential feature of mental acts (Brentano, 1929, p. 58) offers a highly plausible analysis of distinctly human cognition. Allport (1993), a neurocognitive scientist, also focused on the active selection and binding together of those aspects of a stimulus array delineating an object as "brought forth" by concept use, but the natural history of human cognition as emergent from an ORN domain awaited the social anthropology of Tomasello (2014, p. 16). That work explicated the basis of reason (CPR, B 574) and of the self-making of rational, moral beings as a cooperative enterprise resting on shared circuits of quasi-stable patterns of neural excitation dynamically attuned to an action-delineated world (Chemero, 2009; Neisser, 1976) in which they live and move and have their being with others. Making sense of such a world, using propositional content (tied to truth and falsity), can then be analysed in terms of the top-down influence of discursive rules and practices governing the use of concepts (Gillett, 2008) so that human cognition is discursive (CPR, B 93). For instance, a mark on the sand might be seen as the imprint of a foot belonging to a living human being through a judgement <that is a footprint> which abstracts a characteristic pattern from the stimulus array and frames a thought that could be true or false. That cognitive work draws on rule-governed skills mapping the stimulus layout onto propositional content by using re-entrant relations between neurocognitive maps formed within discursive practices "around here" (Edelman, 1992). Our animal cousins do not have access to such things, but may draw on other associative mechanisms to potentiate behaviour in their own ways.

Thought therefore forges a series of links between a present situation and others in a discursively structured system (Kant, CPR, B74) that connects things happening now with things distinct in space and time. The relevant cognitive abilities are associative—causally linked to our sensori-motor interactions, but also discursively—linked to abstractions shaped by human discourse (Harre & Gillett, 1994). They use semantic modes of interaction (Knott, 2012), to learn techniques that become second nature to us, and lock us into norms of truth and falsity.

Concepts unify representations in a communicable way that is inherently multi-perspectival and embedded in the human world (Tomasello, 1999). Thus, during my walk along the beach, a mark in the sand, the breaking of the waves, the gathering clouds indicating a forthcoming storm, the feeling of sand squeaking under my feet, the intense green of the jungle, and so on, all appear in different cognitive maps. That flexible and selective appreciation of my environment rests on various theme-context or figure-ground relations as the information presented to me is articulated by certain concepts and conceptions—<green>, <blue>, <wave>, <the break of a wave>, <sand>, <the tree>, <the sea>, <the foot-print>, <the making of the footprint>, and so on. This extends my "mental grip" on the world by using perception-action schemata that make me conscious of things not accessible to simpler creatures in the same multiplex way. Thus, when I am conscious of a candle, there is much more to that experience than what is available to a kitten; we could say that there are layers of mental life waiting to be explored by me of which a kitten cannot even dream (Scrooge's lonely Christmas vigil by the light of a cheap candle, for instance).

The complex intentional abilities of human beings are continuous with those of their simpler animal cousins but much richer because of the multiplicity of semantic links that humans (from their diverse perspectives and their rich symbolic world) make between experiences at different times and places. Semantics exploits re-entrant neurocognitive maps arising from the use of signs, a world of causal relations, and the conceptual structure of propositions and, as semantically informed beings, human beings learn to pick out stimulus groupings marked by signs or symbols and construct neural assemblies that can be detached from present context to make links between different situations. Thus the "loss of automaticity" referred to by Hughlings-Jackson results from "re-re-representation" by integration of the neural structures controlling behaviour and the potentially diverse contingencies linked by argument to enrich the possibilities open to the human *psyche* (JHJ, 1887).

Merleau-Ponty mirrors "evolutionary neurology" as he ties together the world, language, and our structures of knowledge:

> The system self-others-world ... taken as an object of analysis is now a mat-
> ter of awakening the thoughts which constitute other people, myself as an
> individual subject and the world as a pole of my perception. ... the mistake
> of critical philosophies is to believe that the thinking subject can ... appro-
> priate without remainder the object of thought, that our being can be
> brought down to our knowledge. (1962, pp. 70–72)

## 4   THE EPISTEMIC SOUL: TRIANGULATION, INTERSUBJECTIVITY, JUDGEMENT, AND KNOWLEDGE

Merleau-Ponty locates human knowledge and experience in an intersubjective culturally inscribed world illuminated by human discourse:

> In the experience of dialogue, there is constituted between the other person
> and myself a common ground; my thought and his are inter-woven into a
> single fabric, my words and those of my interlocutor are called forth ...
> inserted into a shared operation of which neither of us is the creator ... we
> are collaborators for each other in consummate reciprocity. (1962, p. 413)

These aspects of intersubjectivity create a multi-perspectival context
constituting an "object-reflective–normative domain" (Tomasello, 2014,
p. 4) through semantic rules based on triangulating objects, reflecting or
reasoning about them, and correcting each others' mistakes. This forms
the framing context for all our thoughts:

> But can't I imagine that the people around me are automata, lack conscious-
> ness, even though they behave in the same way as usual?—If I imagine it
> now—alone in my room—I see people with fixed looks (as in a trance) going
> about their business—the idea is perhaps a little uncanny. But just try to
> keep hold of this idea in the midst of your ordinary intercourse with others,
> in the street, say! Say to yourself, for example: "The children over there are
> mere automata; all their liveliness is mere automatism." And you will either
> find these words becoming quite meaningless; or you will produce in your-
> self some kind of uncanny feeling, or something of the sort. (PI, #420)

Wittgenstein locates us in an embodied, interconnected stream neurocognitive activity that is "the best candidate ... all things considered" for
the basis of conscious experience (Tye, 1999, p. 718). These manifest subjective aspects of our worldly being with others, resting on techniques and
skills (Wittgenstein, PI II.11) trained in an intersubjective milieu (the key

to developmental psychology but often not discussed in philosophy of mind).

The ORN milieu builds on "those sensible Ideas, which we observe" (Locke, EHU, 444) and our untutored intuitions based on them (often taken as given in empiricism) and modifies our contact with things by deploying cognitive maps (evident, for instance, in the premise that an illusion is qualitatively the same as the real). The dynamic and non-linear processes of human cognition produce experience infused by the effects of Merleau-Ponty's "system self-world-other" which steers us around the real world, the workings of which we incorporate into our experience (thus a smile cannot exist without a cat's head connected to a cat's body not floating in the air, nor can steam come from a kettle with no water in it). Human beings are trained to actively explore and exploit their embodied experience en route to discerning real essence ("the real constitution of any Thing ... the foundation of all those Properties ... combined in and constantly found to coexist with the nominal Essence" [EHU, 442]). The life of the soul and cognitive neuroscience are linked by integrating perception and argument in an adequate understanding of a context illuminated by discourse and multi-perspectivality as the basis of adaptive cognition and action (Science is a highly discursive form of reasoned multi-perspectivality and reveals that, for example, dolphins are mammals like cows, not fish, like sharks, that similarly economic growth is a theory-ridden mathematical abstraction not necessarily a reality).

An understanding of real essence is not only the product of human consciousness and mental life, but should frame our thinking about it by drawing on current knowledge of perception, cognition, and embodied cognitive neuroscience, and discarding illusions based only on how things naively appear (Dennett, 1991; Tye, 1999). On that basis, five desiderata characterise an understanding of a human being as a conscious living soul apt for discerning real essence (in accordance with Dennett's heterophenomenology).[27]

## 5    THE REAL ESSENCE OF CONSCIOUSNESS AND THE HUMAN SOUL

The real essence of conscioiusness is therefore multiplex embodying certain aspects:

1. *It should be logically articulate and yield a clear and distinct idea* apt to illuminate the "link" between philosophical analysis, lived human experience, and cognitive neuroscience.

2. *It should reveal the evolutionary significance of consciousness.* Evolution is our best theory of our creaturely characteristics and so should inform our view of human subjectivity and cognition, their adaptive role, the reasons for their persistence, and their maintenance as part of human nature (Griffiths, 1997), as Robinson, an Aristotelian, remarks:

> [B]ehaviour is not explicable solely in terms of cause-effect regularities. Rather, it becomes necessary to consider the entire history of the organism; its innate and acquired modes of adaptation; the part played in its behaviour in the overall success of the organism and its species. (1989, p. 50)

3. *It should ground the "reality principle"* (Freud, 1986, p. 221), whereby consciousness obeys constraints of reason not applicable to non-conscious aspects of the psyche. All mental states are, arguably, causal states (en)actively or passively generated in the subject, but the conscious ego is manifest through self-presentation in the ORN domain and therefore open to appraisal or assessment according to canons of reason (doxastic and orectic) questions that inform our cognitive grip on the world: "What is really going on here?" "Is what I believe true?" "Is that a thought on which I ought to act?" "Is that a suitable object of desire?" These questions normatively adjust the enactive processes linking consciousness, intersubjectivity, and the cultural norms of reason and argument

4. *It should explain a "critters like us" intuition.* Imagine the following thought experiment: human beings design an explorer robot or Zoid, Zac (a bit like C3PO), with sensors translating the effects of environmental conditions or events into a simulation of characteristic human reactions so as to test alien environments on our behalf. Thus, if Zac touches something hot or acidic, it says, "Ouch, its burning my skin" or "Uh-Oh, its eating into me!" It is plausible that we could get concerned about him and say, for instance, "Get him out of there. Can't you see the poor guy is hurting bad!"

We might dismiss this reaction, but given that Zac is like a human being in functional respects despite not being made like us, what justifies that response? Is it a kind of biomolecular chauvinism because Zac is not protoplasm? But imagine Zac saying, after a highly "toxic" (to us) encounter, "Well; that sure was something!

Don't worry it doesn't hurt and I can fix myself up but you guys should not come here." This comment makes Zac seem to be conscious in some of the ways we are and to be responsive to us in a way somewhat like moral concern, but do things "hurt" him and can we meaningfully ask, how does he feel, *inter alia*, about us, his "callous" human controllers? The "critters like us" intuition inclines us to not believe that there is anything it is like to be Zac, but perhaps we need further analysis and exploration of the "real" links between our nature, human consciousness, responsivity, and like-us-ness so as to properly assess our "moral" concern for him.

5. *The account should clarify the link between being conscious in a human-like way and inclusion in our moral community.* Responsibility for action and consciousness of what one is doing, along with a vulnerability to and awareness of harm and suffering, provoke our sympathy and moral concern. A related puzzle concerns mental content and genuine rule-following. A genuine rule follower obeys, as we do, shared rules, because they *are* rules, rather than just conforming to them by exhibiting dispositions or regularities of behaviour that extensionally coincide with rule-following behaviour (possibly consistent with another rule entirely [or a "bent" rule]).[28] A genuine rule follower attends to the rule as a reason for acting in the way s/he does. Moral rules are like that—we follow them intentionally and variably intelligently, given the embedded consideration for others they embed. Being rule governed in that way and for that reason makes a creature one of us—conscious in a fully human way and a proper object of attributions of freedom and resentment.[29]

Second nature is therefore linked to the human soul in that both are internally related to embodied subjectivity, enactive self-formation, reasoning, our vulnerable and appetitive (or creaturely) nature, and our practices of rule-following (Winch, 1958). We gather and act on information that has meaning or significance for us because we participate in human praxis shaping ourselves and our responses to the world according to its norms. Thus the "true internal constitution" (in Locke's sense) of our intellect rests on the neuroscience of sensori-motor coupling and its human integration with our adaptation to discourse and being with others.

## 6    Recap on Chapter 2

An active embodied theory of the human soul as shaped in a distinctly human world can be discerned in philosophical writing from Aristotle to current phenomenology. A neo-Aristotelian concept of second nature as a key to the soul informs anti-reductive strands in culturally informed neurophilosophy and discursive psychology. The enactive global (neurocognitive) workspace model of human consciousness yields a theory of cognition as exploratory and self-making so that human beings become richly responsive and finely aware of being-in-the-world-with-others.[30] Human agency (the active intellect) is seen both in perception and cognition, for instance, in the shift from merely watching the birds in the sky to searching for an albatross in a flock of gulls; here active perception is infused by knowledge based on communication and shared participation in a contingent world to imbue experience with significance through human practices of meaning-making by abstraction, distinction, and conceptualisation, dictating that, for instance, an albatross is not a gull.

The subpersonal natural processes (not mechanisms) of the human soul actively use conceptual content to create a neurocognitive workspace through "a reverberating circuit including frontal areas and perceptual areas, and ... working memory" partially shaped "by the close participation of speech" (Luria, 1973, p. 93).

### Notes

1. Mercier and Sperber (2011).
2. Davidson (2001).
3. CPR B848ff.
4. This is explored in Gillett (1992, esp. Chap. 4).
5. Wittgenstein, *On Certainty*, #402.
6. Inquiries we have as *De Anima* (hereinafter DA).
7. DA, 430a16.
8. It is a key feature of embodied cognition theory (Chemero, 2009; Thompson & Varela, 2001) and the product of neural integration between practically and symbolically attuned assemblies (JHJ, e.g. 1887).
9. Aristotle distinguishes human from animal thought in terms of truth and falsity (DA, 427b12ff).
10. The space of reasons is a sustained focus of McDowell's work (1994, 1998), and the proper role of philosophy is a preoccupation of both Frege and Wittgenstein, both of whom reject the idea that logic merely follows the dispositions of human psychology (a doctrine known as "psychologism").

11. The relation is explored in relation to concepts and consciousness in Gillett (1992, 2014).
12. Merleau-Ponty (1962, p. 157).
13. Kant's *Critique of Pure Reason* (CPR) "discursive" is not further defined and evokes the Greek grammaticos ...
14. Frege (1977, p. 4).
15. This will be discussed in Chap. 2.
16. The conceptually distinct rendering is in the Hugh Lawson-Tancred translation.
17. Wittgenstein uses "grammatical" to reflect the origins of logic in correct use of language (PI ## 90; 111) and thereby echoes an ancient Greek usage.
18. The concept of sedimentation is found in Merleau-Ponty (1962, p. 164ff).
19. McDowell (1998, p. P185-5).
20. McDowell (1998, p. 188).
21. McDowell (1998, p. 179).
22. McDowell (1998, p. 183).
23. NE 1103a20–25.
24. Merleau-Ponty (1973, pp. 12, 14, 16, 17, 25, 31).
25. Wood (2003).
26. Chemero uses the term "bringing forth" to denote the fact that something actual, not just ideal, is introduced.
27. This term is used in Dennett (1991).
28. The idea of a bent rule is a problem generated if there is no categorical state that ensures that a performance will always conform to what we intuitively regard as following the rule (Kripke, 1982; Gillett, 2003).
29. Strawson (1974). I have discussed this link in "'Ought' and Well-being" (Gillett, 1993).
30. Nussbaum, discussed in a chapter in *Love's Knowledge* (1990).

## REFERENCES AND BIBLIOGRAPHY

Adams, F., Drebushenko, D., Fuller, G., & Stecker, R. (1990). Narrow content: Fodor's folly. *Mind & Language, 5*(3), 214–229.
Allport, A. (1993). Visual attention. In M. I. Posner (Ed.), *Foundations of cognitive science* (pp. 631–682). Cambridge, MA: MIT Press.
Baars, B. (2002). The conscious access hypothesis: Origins and recent evidence. *Trends in Cognitive Science, 6*(1), 47–52.
Bartolomeo, P. (2002). The relationship between visual perception and visual mental imagery: A reappraisal of the neuropsychological evidence. *Cortex, 38*(3), 357–378.
Brentano, F. (1874 [1973]). *Psychology from an empirical standpoint* (L. McAlister, Trans.). London: Routledge & Kegan Paul.

Brentano, F. (1929 [1981]). *Sensory and noetic consciousness* (M. Schattle & L. McAlister, Trans.). London: Routledge and Kegan Paul.

Caston, V. (1996). Why Aristotle needs imagination. *Phronesis, 41,* 20–55.

Chemero, A. (2009). *Radical embodied cognitive science.* Cambridge, MA: MIT Press.

Damasio, A. (1996). The somatic marker hypothesis and the possible functions of the prefrontal cortex. *Philosophical Transactions of the Royal Society of London, 351,* 1413–1429.

Davidson, D. (1980). *Essays on actions and events.* Oxford: Clarendon.

Davidson, D. (2001). *Subjective, intersubjective, objective.* Oxford: Oxford University Press.

Dehaene, S., & Naccache, L. (2001). Towards a cognitive neuroscience of consciousness: Basic evidence and a workspace framework. *Cognition, 79,* 1–37.

Dennett, D. (1991). *Consciousness explained.* London: Penguin.

Dreyfus, H., & Taylor, C. (2015). *Retrieving realism.* Cambridge, MA: Harvard University Press.

Edelman, G. (1992). *Bright air, brilliant fire: On the matter if the mind.* London: Penguin.

Evans, G. (1982). *The varieties of reference.* Oxford: Clarendon.

Freeman, W. J. (2015). Mechanism and significance of global coherence in scalp EEG. *Current Opinion in Biology, 23,* 199–205.

Frege, G. (1977). *Logical investigations* (P. Geach, Trans. & Ed.) Oxford: Blackwell.

Frege, G. (1980). *Translations from the philosophical writings of Gottlob Frege* (P. Geach & M. Black, Eds.). Oxford: Blackwell.

Freud, S. (1986). *The essentials of psychoanalysis* (J. Strachey, Trans.). Harmondsworth: Penguin.

Friston, K. (2010). The free energy principle: A unified brain theory? *Nature Reviews/Neuroscience, 11,* 127–134.

Gallagher, S. (2005). *How the body shapes the mind.* Oxford: Oxford University Press.

Gillett, G. (1992). *Representation, meaning and thought.* Oxford: Clarendon.

Gillett, G. (1993). Ought and wellbeing. *Inquiry, 36,* 287–306.

Gillett, G. (1997). Husserl, Wittgenstein and the snark. *Philosophy and Phenomenological Research, LVII,* 331–350.

Gillett, G. (2008). *Subjectivity and being somebody: Human identity and neuroethics* (St Andrews Series on Philosophy and Public Affairs). Exeter: Imprint Academic.

Gillett, G. (2014). Concepts, consciousness and counting by pigeons. *Mind, 123,* 1147–1153.

Gillett, G., & Liu, S. (2012). Free will and Necker's cube: Reason, language and top-down control in cognitive neuroscience. *Philosophy, 87*(1), 29–50.

Gillett, G., & McMillan, J. (2001). *Consciousness and intentionality.* Amsterdam: John Benjamins.

Griffiths, P. (1997). *What emotions really are.* Chicago: University of Chicago Press.

Haldane, J. (1992). Aquinas and the active intellect. *Philosophy, 67,* 199–210.

Harre, R., & Gillett, G. (1994). *The discursive mind.* London: Sage.

Hughlings Jackson, J. (1887). Remarks on the evolution and dissolution of the nervous system. *British Journal of Psychiatry, 33,* 25–48.

Hume, D. (1740 [1969]). *A treatise of human nature* (E. Mossner, Ed.). London: Penguin.

Hurford, J. R. (2003). The neural basis of predicate-argument structure. *Behavioral and Brain Sciences, 26,* 261–316.

Hurley, S. (1998). *Consciousness in action.* Cambridge, MA: Harvard University Press.

Husserl, E. (1950 [1999]). *Cartesian meditations* (D. Cairns, Trans.). Dordrecht: Kluwer.

Husserl, E. (1954 [1970]). *The crisis of European sciences and transcendental phenomenology* (D. Carr, Trans.). Chicago: Northwestern University Press.

Husserl, E. (1982). *Ideas pertaining to a pure phenomenology and to a phenomenological philosophy* (F. Kersten, Trans.). The Hague: Martinus Nijhoff.

Jacquette, D. (2004). *The Cambridge companion to Brentano.* Cambridge, UK: Cambridge University Press.

Kim, J. (2010). *Essays in the metaphysics of mind.* Oxford: Oxford University Press.

King, J. R., Jacobo, D., Faugeras, F., et al. (2013). Information sharing in the brain indexes consciousness in noncommunicative patients. *Current Biology, 23,* 1914–1919.

Knott, A. (2012). *Sensorimotor cognition and natural language syntax.* Cambridge, MA: MIT Press.

Kozma, R., Davies, J., & Freeman, W. J. (2012). Synchronized minima in ECoG power at frequencies between beta-gamma oscillations disclose cortical singularities in cognition. *Journal of Neuroscience and Neuroengineering, 1*(1), 11.

Kripke, S. (1982). *Wittgenstein on rules and private language.* Oxford: Blackwell.

Luria, A. R. (1973). *The working brain.* Harmondsworth: Penguin.

McDowell, J. (1994). *Mind and world.* Cambridge, MA: Harvard University Press.

McDowell, J. (1998). *Mind, value and reality.* Cambridge, MA: Harvard University Press.

Mercier, H., & Sperber, D. (2011). Why do humans reason? Arguments for an argumentative theory. *Behavioural and Brain Sciences, 34,* 57–111.

Merleau-Ponty, M. (1962). *The phenomenology of perception* (C. Smith, Trans.). London: Routledge.

Merleau-Ponty, M. (1973). *Consciousness and the acquisition of language* (H. Silverman, Trans.). Chicago: Northwestern University Press.

Neisser, U. (1976). *Cognition and reality.* San Francisco: Freeman.

Neisser, U. (1982). *Memory observed.* San Francisco: W.H. Freeman & Co.

Nussbaum, M. (1990). *Love's knowledge.* Oxford: Oxford University Press.

Rist, J. (1966). Notes on Aristotle De Anima 3.5. *Classical Philology, 61,* 8–20.

Robinson, D. (1989). *Aristotle's psychology.* New York: Columbia University Press.

Sellars, W. (1997). *Empiricism and the philosophy of mind.* Cambridge, MA: Harvard University Press.

Sorabji, R. (1974). Body and soul in Aristotle. *Philosophy, 49,* 63–89.

Strawson, P. (1974). *Freedom and resentment and other essays.* London: Methuen.

Thompson, E., & Varela, F. (2001). Radical embodiment: Neural dynamics and consciousness. *Trends in Cognitive Science, 5*(10), 416–425.

Tomasello, M. (1999). *The cultural origins of human cognition.* Cambridge, MA: Harvard University Press.

Tomasello, M. (2014). *The natural history of human thinking.* Cambridge, MA: Harvard University Press.

Treisman, A. (1996). The binding problem. *Current Opinion in Neurobiology, 6,* 171–178.

Tye, M. (1999). Phenomenal consciousness: The explanatory gap as a cognitive illusion. *Mind, 108,* 705–726.

Winch, P. (1958). *The idea of a social science and its relation to philosophy.* London: Routledge.

Wood, A. (2003). Kant and the problem of human nature. In B. Jacobs & P. Kain (Eds.), *Essays on Kant's anthropology.* Cambridge: Cambridge University Press.

Zahavi, D. (2003). *Husserl's phenomenology.* Stanford, CA: Stanford University Press.

Zahavi, D. (2005). *Subjectivity and selfhood: Investigating the first person perspective.* Cambridge, MA: MIT Press.

# CHAPTER 3

# Evolutionary Neurology and the Human Soul

**Abstract** A nervous system configured by intersubjectivity and a grasp of the distinction between truth and falsity shape our neural function so that we sense, perceive, cognise, and act in ways that elaborate sensori-motor activity to fit us for cognitive function under norms of truth and falsity conveyed by and linked to speech or "propositionising." The resulting self-formation fits us for a world in which meaningful symbolism and normatively constrained communication imposes truth and falsity and depth as the basis of a well-organised intellect. Thus our sensori-motor and language-related neural functions are fitted for the joint demands of the natural world and the socio-political (or discursive) world through triply responsive neurocognitive assemblies shaped in human cognitive development and underpinning human consciousness, thought, and action.

**Keywords** Evolutionary neurology • Propositionising • Cognition and being-in-the-world-with-others

> *"Is there any other point to which you would wish to draw my attention?"*
> *"To the curious incident of the dog in the night-time."*
> *"The dog did nothing in the night-time."*
> *"That was the curious incident," remarked Sherlock Holmes*

© The Author(s) 2018                                              45
G. Gillett, *From Aristotle to Cognitive Neuroscience*,
https://doi.org/10.1007/978-3-319-93635-2_3

A workable philosophy of the soul, broadly naturalistic, sees the brain as a complex dynamic system that accumulates habitual and structured ways of responding to situations, generating predictions about the world and looking for familiar stimulus patterns apt for a particular construction of the present state of affairs. Oscillations linking cortex to subcortical centres such as the thalamus and hippocampus effectively create "a complex structure of feedback loops or 're-entrant loops'" (Klimesch, 1999). The non-linear brain dynamics fuelling the predictive brain (Freeman, 2008; Friston, 2010) and its configuring of behaviour unpack the "active intellect" of Aristotle in a way that prefigures embodied cognition theory (Clark, Varela, Thompson, Chemero). The nineteenth-century evolutionary neurology of JHJ and the cognitive neuroscience of Alexandr Luria, Bernard Baars, and Gerald Edelman combine to yield a neo-Aristotelian account of enactive consciousness as a natural phenomenon arising in the human neural network to integrate multiple sources of information arising in a domain of adaptation aided by communication (Tomasello, 2014). That evolutionary framework incorporating what JHJ calls "propositionising" draws on top-down—autopoietic and bottom-up—contingent associative patterns of neural integration supplemented by re-entrant oscillatory loops of cerebral excitation. Melding together the causal flux of (first or raw) nature and the ORN domain of discourse characteristic of the human cognitive niche creates second nature and reveals how the human soul integrates three sources of information—the two poles of individual sensori-motor neural coupling and a discursive order of human communication (structured by semantic connections and argumentation).

The material basis of such behavioural control comprises elements— brain neurones, their dendritic fields and layered neural networks, their connections to the body, and their multiplex neural interconnections— produces highly complex patterns of intra- and interorganismic connectedness. This multiplicity of multiple systems of connectivity and resonance engenders potential shifts in patterns of excitation that are quasi-stable over time and balance relatively robust and settled habitual modes of activity with innovative changes needed for evolving cognitive control[1] (Fig. 3.1).

Neurones pass information between different areas of the brain by receiving excitatory impulses, through synapses, into dendritic trees, forming complex fields that "pass the message on" depending on other coincident excitation and existing connections with other brain centres. The overall effect is to generate dynamic excitation patterns depending on the number of neurones firing in a given area and privileged input

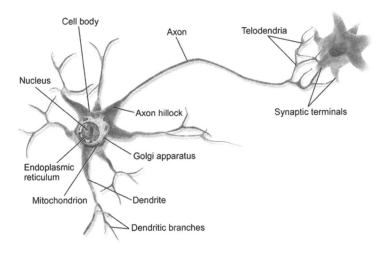

**Fig. 3.1**    The connectivity of brain neurones. Source: http://neurosciencenews.com/files/2014/10/neuron-diagram.jpg

patterns (because of factors like long-term potentiation; Kolb & Whishaw, 1990, p. 873). The "stronger" the connection or likelihood of linking together two cerebral areas (reflecting the level of historically correlated activity), the more the synchrony between the respective dendritic fields (effectively creating a linked cluster of maps capturing features of the environment relevant to the organism). This analogue process reflects coincidence/temporal association of messages (as reinforced by rewards or avoidance of expected negative contingencies) and the frequency with which the relevant connections are made in cumulative experience. These emergent patterns of connectivity are underpinned by "Hebb's law" (*neurones that fire together wire together*) and Thorndike's law of effect (*a behaviour's frequency is altered by its positive and negative effects*).[2] Firing patterns in an established and well-functioning behavioural control system therefore generate attractors for neural network activity that generates responses properly adapted to a domain (e.g. patterns picking up perceptual cues evoking a behavioural technique that makes food available, taking part in a dance or conversation that is familiar and thereby accessing social and interactional rewards).

In fact, neurones act as selective excitatory conduits between fields of influence—the (dendritic) field, where information (including appetitive information) is gathered, and the (axonal) field, where it has diverse effects on another (field-like) area or centre of connectivity. This connectivity is seen in anatomical depictions of neurones.

The neurones depicted are from the cerebral cortex; they connect information through the networks of arborising connections in diverse fields of cerebral activity. The resulting neuronal assemblies confer plasticity by gathering diverse information from neurones, each with their own pattern of environmental "pick-up," enabling multi-factorial analogue processing and time-moderated coordination of information in sequences, coupled with a context of action and interaction (perhaps, for humans, at the level of the signifier as part of a symbol-using network). The connectivity patterns characteristically use rhythms of excitation (e.g. at alpha frequency) to establish new connections and different frequencies of oscillation (theta frequency) to engage more settled links between disparate brain areas, creating, for example, long-term-memory-related functions (Klimesch, 1999). The establishment of such dynamic oscillation patterns between distributed assemblies of neurones and their dendritic fields underpins the ongoing work of extracting significance by the predictive brain as it searches the environment for patterns related to established behavioural interventions (Freeman, 2000, 2008). The bottom-up and top-down integration of neuronal function within neural systems subserves natural purposes in the animal and human brain (the latter being linked to symbolism and the ORN domain). These processes generate an active and growing set of acquired capacities ready for use in "the global workspace" (Baars, 2002) that unified matrix of connections allows the active coordination used in semantically informed, conscious, cooperative human activity to serve cooperative ends/purposes as human souls learn to negotiate the moral community that has formed them (Kant's "a kingdom of ends").

## 1    JOHN HUGHLINGS-JACKSON AND EVOLUTIONARY NEUROLOGY

John Hughings-Jackson's evolutionary neurology (1887) focused on the integration and coordination of sensori-motor functions, arguing human neural processes could yield a phylogenetic and ontogenetic basis for psychological life (1887, p. 39) and that breakdowns in that integration and coordination lead to neurological and psychological disorders. He argued that integration and coordination represent "impressions and movements of all parts of the body ... in most complex ... combinations ... triply indirectly" to organise human behaviour (1887, p. 29); "triply indirectly" because successive layers of input override simple reflex-like connections (whereby an input automatically elicits a stereotyped output). Evolved neural function uses diverse sources of information (external or intra-cerebral, e.g. cortico-subcortical, cortico-cortical, or cortico-subcortico-cortical) to moderate an organism's responses. This process can be thought of as the use of re-entrant links between diverse cognitive maps to construct multi-faceted attunement between organism and environment by creating "reservoirs of energy" and "resisting positions" to (1887, p. 32) produce the "intricate co-coordinations of impressions and movements" (p. 34) we call cognition. Thus the brain, including the cortex, builds multi-level platforms of connectedness as "the substrata of the most elaborate mental operations" (p. 35), the "physical basis of mind" (p. 36) assemblies which enable a holistic, layered, and neurally distributed "seat of consciousness" resulting from an active process of neural configuration and reconfiguration; this is the machinery (or vehicle) of the soul.

JHJ's denial that "consciousness is a function of the brain" (p. 37) must therefore be interpreted in the light of his doctrine of concomitance (p. 38), which avoids both Cartesian interactionism and mind-brain identity and preserves Aristotle's conceptual distinctness that some have simplified to suit the metaphysics of supervenience. Concomitance allows for top-down non-linear dynamics between the highest levels of neural integration (attuned to an interpersonal and discursive field) and more basic stimulus-driven or quasi-automatic processes (the coupling of embodied cognition theory). This theory recognises "ascending adaptation" whereby its higher levels, through autopoietic or enactive effects on lower-level assemblies (Gillett & Liu, 2016), fit the human organism to participate in "the kingdom of ends." Complex, field-to-field, dynamic, and oscillatory circuits thus imply that "the whole body is the organ of mind" (p. 39). That thesis blocks reductive moves from natural purposes and the non-linear dynamics of discursive effects on neural function to linear causal chains at lower levels such that "mental" and "conscious" are terms denoting holistic and integrated neural functions putting us in contact with the human world (1887, p. 34). That relation is influenced by propositional (symbolic) content as used by real people in their doings and their "personal referential language" (Snowdon, 2014, p. 175). Unconscious mental states indicate "lowest nervous arrangements of the highest centres which have no attendant psychical states ... yet lead to next level activities ... [with] attendant psychical states." JHJ's view here is therefore similar to Searle's analysis of the mind (1992, p. 151ff), where "aspectual shapes," made explicit in Frege's "cognitive significance" or Evans' "ways of thinking," inflect our responses to real things and our dealings with them (Brentano's "reism" or Heidegger's focus on our dealings with things as the basis of thinking).[3]

JHJ illustrates unconscious processing by discussing epileptic states of automatism where "the patient is 'unconscious,' and acts elaborately"(1887, p. 40) as if performing an intentional act—such as mending a fishing net despite being unconscious of his context. The example shows that even the lower-level sensori-motor coupling is complex, dynamic, and non-linear (through continuous reciprocal causation) such that "concomitance" between nervous and mental states (the latter shaped by engagement in personal referential practices) preserves the integrity of speech and thought and neurophysiological explanations without any "hybrid" descriptions. JHJ uses this term for the illicit mixing of psychological and neural terms (e.g. secondary visual cortex alerts the motor system to target movements). This is not supervenience (Kim, 2010) because mental phenomena such as "sensations, volitions, ideas, and emotions" do not cause physical states—a thesis that would "imply disbelief in the doctrine of conservation of energy" (p. 40) rather:

> [N]ervous arrangements discharged during any mental process no doubt represent the whole body (Integration), although some part of it most (specialisation); during visual perception those discharged represent most especially the retinal and ocular parts of the body. (p. 42n)

Mental phenomena reflect (are abstracted from) our "triply indirect" responsiveness inflected not only by sensori-motor coupling (Kant's purposive teleological flow) tied to embodiment but also by propositionising—an abstraction from language use. The various insanities and dissolutions of this integrated activity are breakdowns of the dynamic re-re-representation and control coordinating human behaviour (pp. 47–48):

> [O]n the lowest level ... (1) centres for simplest movements of the limbs become evolved in the highest centres into the physical bases of volition;

what on the lowest level (2) are centres for simple reflex actions of eyes and hands are evolved in the highest centres into the physical bases of visual and tactual ideas; what on the lowest level are (3) centres for movements of the tongue palate lips, &C., as concerned in eating swallowing &c., are ... evolved into the physical bases of words, symbols serving us during abstract reasoning. (4) What on the lowest level are centres representing the circulatory, respiratory, and digestive movements are evolved ... into the physical bases of emotions. (p. 48)

Here the embodied, active, human neural function is seamlessly merged into the functions of second nature, whereby reason organises precise responses to new combinations of things (JHJ, 1879, p. 218) through the service of words and their combinatorial and symbolic structure itself woven together with the flow of embodied life. The astounding sensori-motor coupling in the "Bilbo's meal" sequence of *The Hobbit* shows us a non-conceptual precursor of our shared circuits; the dwarves, having "crashed" Bilbo's home for a meal, clean up the mess with blinding perceptuo-motor precision and coordination, throwing, catching, and using skills built from shared circuits of sensori-motor control (Hurley, 2008). The job is done in the blink of an eye. Their interactive responsiveness reveals layers of contextual attunement, exemplifying a level of complexity analogous to the intricate and nuanced conversation and social techniques described by Jane Austen.

Hebb's law, together with Thorndike's law of effect, supports this account of neural evolution and the concept of *affordances*—opportunities or threats for an organism indicated by (possibly non-obvious) features of stimulus arrays in an ecological domain (Chemero, 2003). For example: certain skin colours of fruit signal nutritive content—an opportunity of nourishment at little cost—and the concept *ripeness* uses them to help a human organism avoid the costs of consuming unripe fruit (extra work, possible disabling gut pain, and poor digestion). In a related way, one can imagine finding a human skull (unconsciously responding with fear or alarm): that weaves into the thought complex, "a human being died near here is there lethal danger nearby?" And skulls can be relocated, carrying their associative significance with them, fulfilling a symbolic or intentional role (as in skull totems). Portable "mobility of association" is an essential feature of symbolic communication and it vastly expands our ability to guide others by transmitting messages expressing diverse perspectives.

Affordances render stimulus patterns as significant to us, perhaps by association with Damasio's "somatic markers" (or Thorndike's "reinforcers"), affective bodily states that influence our behaviour and decisions. The human mind, for JHJ, is based on a combination of increasing sensorimotor facility and "propositionising" so as to potentiate an expanding, cumulative, temporally distributed, and elaborated set of adaptations attuned to natural conditions and the human ecosphere. Mental life is formed in that milieu, and is prominent in human ethology and conscious mental life as an enactive means to self-transformation.

An overall picture emerges of a purposive, integrated human organism actively using a system that gathers and orders information of increasing complexity available through a neural network of interconnected dendritic trees forming complex maps and linked to other such maps to modulate a fine-tuned adaptation to an environment pervaded by discourse. Human beings subsume, co-opt, and recruit various neurocognitive capacities built on these re-entrant associative assemblies so as to embody forward-looking (predictive-modelling-based) cognition (Thompson & Varela, 2001). Human second nature shapes desires and expectations in ways foreshadowed, in philosophy, by Aristotle, Kant, Husserl, Wittgenstein, and Merleau-Ponty, and, in neuroscience, by Edelman, Friston, Varela, and Thompson. Taken together, we have an active embodied theory of the human soul in which "ascending adaptation" to a moral community emerges from a developed account of neural evolution, consciousness, and language.

The idea that *cognition is anticipation* treats cognition as comprising forward-planning systems (Barsalou, Breazeal, & Smith, 2007; Rosen, 1985) and implies that any organism elaborates an internal model of itself in its environment and generates predictions about future situations and the challenges and opportunities likely to arise. The resulting "hodological map" detects affordances based on non-obvious stimulus patterns encountered "around here" and generates perceptuo-motor cycles of "retention and protention" as the basis of mental continuity. Human beings add their collective, communicated experience into the mix so that no moment of experience is self-contained and disconnected—attention and intention are based on the thinker's retention of associations between aspects of human situations and the symbolically enhanced "anticipation" that informs and shapes our activity.

Human consciousness and our second nature develop together, keying us into the world in ways explored by post-structuralist (or structural

empiricist)[4] analyses of (i) layered sensori-motor coupling and (ii) propositional or communicative influences on neural assemblies. That multiplicity generates interwoven neurocognitive "maps," organising human
activity in sport, social life, art, symbolism, and music (where the connections result from meaning-infused praxis). Our distinctive human engagement with other human beings therefore generates adaptive repertoires
based on chains of thought (e.g. *I see what he is doing; the effect of his action
will be lethal; I must prevent the murder.* or, *I see his plan, I doubt she does,
but a remark like "a palpable hit" should tip her off*).

## 2   JOHN HUGHLINGS-JACKSON, NEURAL INTEGRATION, AND CONSCIOUSNESS

JHJ does not localise consciousness (or favour modularity in neural function), but double dissociation—derived from the localising agenda—highlights the ascending adaptation of human beings from an animal level to
the level of discursive psychological function.

### 2.1   Double Dissociation and Neuropsychology

The neuropsychological principle of double dissociation is used to uncover
contributory elements in complex human mental functions normally integrated and manifest holistically. These complex and interwoven skills are
affected by damage to contributory brain circuits and systems in different,
even non-overlapping, ways so that functional components can be posited
which, though normally entangled, have different neural bases (Parkin,
1996, pp. 9–14). For instance, the visual recognition of animals may be
affected by damage in cortical area A, but recognition of inanimate objects
may be intact and vice versa if cortical area B is damaged; we can infer that
the two functions have distinct neural substrates. In fact, many cognitive
skills are like that and, therefore, even if "double dissociation" is open to
serious objections (Van Orden, Pennington, & Stone, 2001), it helps
analyse brain injuries as "experiments of nature" dissecting the apparently
seamless web of cognition. The neurology of consciousness is a case in
point: *locked-in syndrome* (LiS) is a condition in which a person is fully
conscious (and more or less cognitively intact) but unable to act or communicate (Gillett, 2004, p. 182); a *vegetative state* (VS), by contrast, is a
state in which patients are unconscious, although input-output systems are

intact (Jennet & Plum, 1972). LiS spares the cerebral cortex with its inter-connecting re-entrant maps of integrated function and VS destroys that interconnected "workspace." We infer that human consciousness is linked to activity in the complex integrative functions of the neocortex and the global workspace it creates (Baars, 2002; JHJ, 1887) and LiS disrupts the interface with the world and others.

## 2.2    Complexity and Consciousness

JHJ analysed consciousness as an amalgam of will, memory, reason, and emotion; all higher-level patterns of sensori-motor integration and inter-connected responsivity are bound together by oscillations of excitation (Chemero, 2009; Freeman, 2008). Alpha- and theta-frequency synchro-nies construct the dynamic neural hyper-assemblies integrating high-level neurocognitive adaptation. Manifest as intentions, learning, problem solv-ing, and emotive responses engendering dynamic interaction with the world, these neuronal assemblies underpin well-practised routines or skills, comprising a "flow" in cognition and behaviour (Csiksentmihalyi, 1990). These flows may or may not give rise to explicit memories and form the basis of "propositionising," but they are all resonant with affordances. Propositionising, where it operates, is explicitly engaged with "structures of nervous energy organised according to word meanings" (JHJ, 1878, p. 323) so that, as Luria notes, "higher mental processes are formed and take place on the basis of speech activity" (1973, pp. 93–94) and the neu-rocognitive assemblies (NcAs) arising from our learning, mastery, and enjoyment of new skills. Words, as symbolic and flexibly related to natural states of affairs, lead to extensive offline possibilities for configuring and re-configuring the internal connections between speech and the real-world situations, giving words their life (Wittgenstein, PI, ##95, 432). Propositionising therefore links human thought and action to an intersub-jective, multi-perspectival (Tomasello, 1999), or "objective" (Davidson, 2001) world of argument (Mercier & Sperber, 2011); in short, in "a space of reasons" (McDowell, 1994; Sellars, 1997) constructed by human beings.

Human consciousness therefore uses rich and inclusive neural associa-tions (including those furnished by speech) to elaborate cognitive control. It is already "the least automatic" and most highly integrated animal activ-ity (JHJ, 1887, p. 41), but in the space of reasons it becomes richly informed by the communicated experience of a human group. That highest level of function is mediated by the frontal lobes—the "highest motor centres" (1887, p. 30) as the neural basis of actively directed intellectual activity that is most inclusive of information from a holistic distributed network of top-down and bottom-up processes dynamically interacting in a non-linear way, but not as a (local or "Cartesian") locus of subjectivity (Dennett, 2003; Gillett, 2008).

Memory, emotion, and reasoning resonate in the global workspace through oscillations reflected in chaotic and synchronous phases of EEG activity (Klimesch, 1999) as the human soul builds and rebuilds its patterns of cognitive integration drawing on sensori-motor association patterns and discursive meanings (Freeman, 2008) to become triply responsive to

1. sensori-motor couplings and world-involving problem-solving routines,
2. limbic and orbito-frontal activity (the neural basis of self-directed emotive and memory functions), and
3. patterns in left hemispheric speech centres (organised by "propositionising"/language use) and therefore "grammar" (Wittgenstein).

The result is a repertoire of goal-directed activity (mediated by dorsolateral prefrontal areas) integrated in time under holistic constraints arising from oscillatory top-down activity that is anatomically distributed (Dennett, 1991; Freeman, 1994; Gillett & Liu, 2012; Spitzer, 1999, p. 124ff; Thompson & Varela, 2001) and collated in the ventromedial prefrontal areas (Damasio, 1996). That integration, as JHJ claimed, includes: (1) *will* or conscious self-coordination of action; (2) *memory* (a "catch-all" term for a whole series of processes that include learning, autobiographical memory, source memory, and semantic memory, all using past experience to inform present behaviour [Gillett, 2008, p. 84ff]); (3) *emotional resonance* within oneself and with others, aided by "gut feelings" and "speech" for JHJ (and Luria), and reactively shaping "centres whereby the organism as a whole is adjusted to an (inter-personal, shared) environment" (JHJ, 1887, p. 34); (4) *reasoning* and a propositional structure so pervasive that even the loss of ready use of words (e.g. from damage to the dominant hemisphere) only causes a partial dissolution of our highest level of soul-life, with some service of words remaining (JHJ, 1878, 1879, p. 222).

## 2.3    Propositionising, Language, and the Soul

Language function is a set of routines linked to symbols poetically and analytically so as to talk but also deploy a range of semiotic associations informing high-level adaptation: "words are required for thinking, for most of our thinking at least but the speechless man is not wordless; there is an automatic or unconscious service of words" (1878, p. 323). In fact, the fittest or strongest associations (1879, p. 341) between a situation and human functions often use words because of their infinitely creative potential (Chomsky, 2006) and multiplex use in devising new ways of dealing with things learnt from others; "an utterance is or is not a proposition according to how it is used" (1879, p. 210) and "superiority of speech is precision of application to new relations of things" (1879, p. 218). Thus adaptations aided by speech, formed and refined within the ORN domain (Tomasello), are so human that Heidegger describes a human being as *Zoon logon Echon* (living being of the word, 1953, H25), a being who incorporates through autopoietic/enactive self-configuration the lessons that shape human second nature to fit us for "the space of reasons," our cognitive niche (Pinker, 2010).

Speech and language engender ideas because "[t]o speak is not simply to utter words, it is to propositionise (1878, p. 311)," representing a peak in adaptational ascent. Wittgenstein's claim that "meaning is use" (PI, #43) and Luria's close participation of speech in all "higher mental processes" incorporate the "complex of cues and connections" constituting the meaning of a word (Luria, 1973, p. 306), infusing the human soul with shared ways of dealing with actual states of affairs or occasions for action as they are illuminated by language in its pragmatic or problem-solving role (Vygotsky, 1962, p. 106). That semantic basis for thought is central in a neo-Fregean analysis (of the type underpinning Evans' GC) and it brings to the fore the transfer of learning based on communication about *objects of reference* (identifiable and re-identifiable in different encounters) and *general predicates* jointly comprising the sense/*Sinn* or propositional content capturing the facts of a situation able to be communicated and reasoned about (TLP, 1.1). This analysis implies a world-involving or embodied theory of thought (Knott, 2012; Noe, 2009) and science (Vygotsky, 1962, p. 116) linking our dealings with things to the cooperative development of world-related skills (both pragmatic and cognitive).

Even subconscious, or relatively inarticulate, human reactions and responses, based on experiences with others, reflect the "service of words" as neurocognitive "markers" (Blackburn, 1984, p. 138) making links and unifying (possibly distributed) neural assemblies bound together within episodes in which human beings talk about what happens and form episodic memories. The memory traces of those episodes capture and make available (in long-term and procedural memory) the results of dynamic perceptuo-motor cycles (Klimesch, 1999; Knott, 2012) based on regularities of interest to human beings (Wittgenstein PI, #570). Words and concepts thus inform and refine our thinking about our shared world. In that way "propositionising" links post-Fregean analytical philosophy (e.g. Evans, Campbell, Cussins) to discursive psychology, argument, and non-linear brain dynamics (Freeman, 2008; Hurford, 2003) because speech is "a tool for intellectual activity and ... a method of regulating or organizing human mental processes" (Luria, 1973, p. 307). Our stories, and what we can and do tell about the world, are the keys to our shared lives (Dennett, 1991). Thus JHJ's neurological insights, often neglected by Anglo-American analytical philosophers and cognitive neuroscientists, but developed by European thinkers, including Lev Vygotsky and Luria, his pupil, therefore bridge from contemporary cognitive neuroscience to a philosophical analysis of the human soul in terms of consciousness and cognition (Franz & Gillett, 2011; Gillett & Franz, 2014).

## 3   EDELMAN AND ECOLOGY

### 3.1   Edelman: Neuronal Group Selection, Concepts, and Consciousness

The establishment during ontogeny of quasi-stable, interconnected neural assemblies through dynamic intra-cerebral oscillation during learning and encoding is part of the process that captures memories based on the significance of an event. A "neurocognitive map" is generated by the resulting network of assemblies and recalls Edelman's (1992) theory of neuronal group selection (TNGS), in which the brain gives rise to supra-neuronal structures (here linked to the higher-order sensori-motor and discursive integration underpinning second nature):

> The three tenets of the TNGS ... are concerned with how the brain is set up during development, how patterns of responses are then selected from this

anatomy during experience, and how re-entry, a process of signalling between the resulting maps of the brain, give rise to behaviorally important functions. (p. 83)

Edelman identifies maps in visual and association areas generated by the predictive brain according to "the statistics of signal correlations" (p. 90), whereby "learning ... connects categorization to behaviors having adaptive value under conditions of expectancy" (p. 101). The method whereby these NcAs communicate with each other is cerebral synchrony and the non-linear dynamics of intra-cerebral oscillation (Freeman, 2008, 2015) at alpha (working memory) and theta (long-term memory) EEG frequencies; this is the predictive brain forming itself.

Edelman analyses concepts as follows: an animal capable of having concepts identifies a thing or an action on the basis of aptitude for the control of behaviour in a more or less general way. This process interconnects perceptual categorisations, even if apparently unrelated, by grouping the relevant stimulus patterns under categorisations reflected in connectivity patterns in re-entrant maps built during ontogeny (Edelman, 1992, p. 108). We can recall Kant's abstraction as a power of the mind.

Kant characterises this process in terms of functions of unity of representations, linked to Brentano's "three beat" function of perception (Davis, Gillett, & Kozma, 2016), and Evans' GC (1982) aspects of an active view of cognition, with echoes in Edelman's theory and phenomenology:

> The brain areas responsible for concept formation contain structures that categorize, discriminate and recombine the various brain activities occurring in different kinds of global mappings ... according to modality, the presence or absence of movement, and the presence or absence of relationships between perceptual categorizations. (Edelman, 1992, p. 109)

Phenomenological analysis argues that "[c]onsciousness shows intentionality: it is _of_ or _about_ things (cf. Edelman "the soul is, in a sense, its objects) to some extent bound up with volition" because it is linked to "significant indicators to the animal of danger or reward" (1992, pp. 112, 123), as these are encoded or captured by semantic skills: "memory, comprehension and speech production interact in a great variety of ways by reentry" (1992, p. 126). The human self, as already discussed, is adapted to a richly textured world communicated about by multiple observers, each with their own perspective (Tomasello, 1999, p. 56ff), giving human consciousness a distinct cognitive advantage over creatures with more impoverished communication:

> The freeing of parts of conscious thought from the constraints of an immediate present and the increased richness of social communication allow for the anticipation of future states and for planned behaviour. With that ability come the abilities to model the world, to make explicit comparisons and to weigh outcomes. (Edelman, 1992, p. 135)

This theme develops William James' idea that attention is a directed volitional activity "taking possession by the mind, in clear and vivid form, of one out of what seem several simultaneously possible objects or trains of thought" (p. 141). Generating supra-neuronal assemblies that engage with objects of acquaintance (Chemero, 2011, p. 185; James, 1909, p. 11) engenders intentionality that intertwines abstract shared symbolism with actual world encounters and techniques to make human encounters meaningful at many levels (Freeman, 2000).

### 3.2    Ecological Psychology: Gibson, Neisser, and Active Perception

Ulrich Neisser, extending the work of James J. and Eleanor Gibson, developed an ecological theory of the meaningfulness that organises the life of a living and embodied soul:

> [M]ost perceptible objects and events are meaningful. They afford various possibilities for action, carry implications about what has happened or what will happen, belong coherently to a larger context, possess an identity that transcends their simple physical properties. These meanings can be, and are, perceived. (1976, p. 71)

"Afford" and "affordance" arise from the ecological cycle of perceptuomotor schemata arising from an active, *embodied* existence apt for language-related enhancement:

> People move. They turn their heads, shift their bodies, walk to the next room, go to the store, or travel around the world. The nature of perception cannot be understood without talking their mobility into account. (1976, p. 108)

These ecological insights, central to recent discussions of perception and embodied cognition (O'Regan & Noe, 2001), are not a kind of behaviourism (Block, 2001); rather the approach notices an integrated holistic function of the whole organism whereby "re-re-representation" of information at ascending levels of neural connection brings forth "virtual neuro-cognitive objects" (Chemero, 2009, pp. 192–195) that are constantly being updated by intelligent engagement with the real world and, after Hughlings-Jackson, also linked to "propositionising." Kant's power of abstraction and analysis of judgement and Wittgenstein's understanding of the complexity inherent in the linked claims that "we—and our meaning" do not stop "anywhere short of the fact" and "thought can also be of what is not the case" (PI #95) resonate with Aristotle's treatment of imagination and reason. The role of discourse vis-à-vis the predictive brain suggest that communicatively elaborated Gestalts tell us what is going on through a constant multi-layered cognitive structure built on brain synchrony between different areas and their cognitive maps (Freeman, 2008).

Perception, on this account, "is a mode of exploration of the world ... mediated by knowledge, on the part of the perceiver, of what we call sensori-motor contingencies" (O'Regan & Noe, 2001, p. 940). The regularities underpinning this type of knowledge include contingencies emerging from ecological engagement but also from human discourse. Propositional content is abstracted from language games in which one participates so that argument and the disciplined use of reason impose an order on the world emerging from shared adaptation, in which "the crystal purity of logic [is] not ... *a result of investigation* it [is] a requirement" (PI #107). We do not extract from the world a copy of it and find that, lo and behold, it has a logical structure that grounds metaphysics; rather, as Kant and Wittgenstein realised (Chap. 1), we train ourselves to abstract certain general features and defining criteria from our pragmatic and discursive proceedings, guided by "the collective reason of humanity (CJ, 136) and our shared interests (PI #570).

Experience is therefore not an unfolding series of impressions but an interpretive "hodological map" such that one's active relations to the world emerge from and update closely entwined threads woven into an understanding of self and the world: "the world around us ... the world of our desires, our needs and our activities appears to be all furrowed with strait and narrow paths leading to such and such a determinate end" (Sartre, 1971, p. 62)—these paths cognitively structure our being-in-the-world-with-others:

The impression we have of ... a coherent world thus arises through the knitting together of a number of separate sensory and sensory-motor components, making use of visual, vestibular, tactile and proprioceptive information; and in which different behaviors (e.g. reading, grasping, bicycle riding constitute components that adapt independently but each contribute to [that] experience. (O'Regan & Noe, 2001, p. 953)

This embodied theory of perception and consciousness resonates with Aristotle's naturalism and, if supplemented by semiotics or discursive theory (Harre & Gillett, 1994), is convergent with phenomenology, existentialism, and even post-structuralism (whereby the significance we attach to something emerges from overlapping and connected cognitive networks of connections pulled together by *autopoiesis* or self-creation [found in Kant's philosophy of nature]).

4    VARELA AND THOMPSON: AUTOPOIESIS

Autopoiesis (dynamic self-organisation) introduces dynamic systems theory and the following three tenets into cognitive neuroscience:

1.  [U]nderstanding the complex interplay of brain, body and world requires the tools and methods of non-linear dynamical systems theory;
2.  traditional notions of representation [as] computation are inadequate;
3.  traditional decompositions of the cognitive systems into inner functional subsystems or modules ... are misleading. (Thompson & Varela, 2001)

Those tenets undermine the search for neural correlates of consciousness conceived on the basis of supervenience or functional reduction and direct us towards "two way or reciprocal relationships between neural events and conscious activity" so that "the processes crucial for consciousness cut across brain-body-world divisions rather than being brain-bound neural events" (p. 418). Thus the soul, as the form of the living body, is, in part, its objects:

Given that the coupled dynamics of brain, body, and environment exhibit self-organization and emergent processes at multiple levels and that

emergence involves both upward and downward causation, it seems legiti-
mate to conjecture that downward causation occurs at multiple levels ...
including that of conscious cognitive acts in relation to local neural activity.
(2001, p. 421)

The non-linearity, recalls Aristotle's "formal causation," is a valid way
of understanding that the whole configures the parts that make it up, as in
obviously autopoietic systems (like the embryo). There are, no doubt,
micro-mechanisms realising such causation throughout biology, but their
workings (as Kant noted) may not be seen through the lens of mechanistic
explanation, given that the causal nexus is multiplex and probabilistic, and
derives explanatory power from the functioning whole finally achieved
(i.e. quasi-teleologically). Non-linear brain dynamics of the type required
here (Freeman, 2015) is prefigured by Kant: "a thing exists as a natural
purpose if it is ... both *cause and effect of itself*" (CJ, 217) and "parts
should so combine in the unity of a whole that they are reciprocally cause
and effect of each other's form" (CJ, 219–220). However, there is a
caveat, proper to scientific explanation, in that accounts of self-organising
nature must be constructed "without prejudice to the principle of mechan-
ical causality" (p. 226) through which nature can be "mechanically considered ... subject to observation and experiment" (p. 231).

Where Kant sees autopoiesis and natural purposes as part of an inclusive
understanding of nature, as in JHJ's evolutionary account of neural processes that progressively integrate subordinate assemblies to serve the
adaptations of a whole organism to its ecological niche, he realises that we
must set this holism aside and posit mechanisms on which we can experiment to investigate the causal world as a methodological prolegomenon
to scientific investigation.

## 5    CEREBRAL CONNECTIVITY AND NON-LINEAR BRAIN DYNAMICS: CREATING MEANING

The dependence of consciousness on the integration of widespread neuronal assemblies is shown in recent studies of neural activity and consciousness in patients (Dehaene & Changeux, 2011; Dehaene, 2014) recovering
from anaesthesia (King et al., 2013). Figures 3.2 and 3.3 picture this process through weighted mutual symbolic information use in the brain.

The diagram depicts the length and intensity of activation in intra-
cerebral connections at various levels of consciousness and portrays

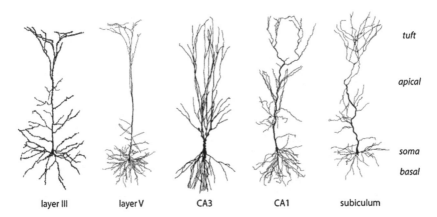

**Fig. 3.2**   The connectivity of motor neurones. Source: http://brainmind.com/ images/PyramidalNeurons.jpg

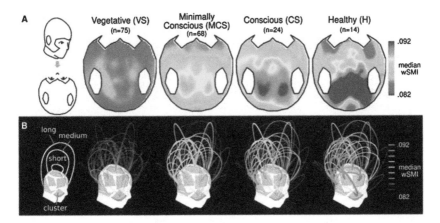

**Fig. 3.3**   Weighted mutual symbolic information (wSMI) increases with consciousness, primarily over centroposterior regions. (A) The median wSMI that each EEG channel shares with all other channels is depicted for each state of consciousness. (B) 120 pairs formed by 16 clusters of EEG channels are depicted as 3D arcs whose height is proportional to the Euclidian distance separating the two clusters. Line colour and thickness are proportional to the mean wSMI shared by the corresponding cluster pair

connected conscious cognitive processing by representing weighted mutual symbolic information (wMSI)—the extent to which different brain areas work together at a given time (as required by the active global workspace model). Here, being consciously focused on a topic or object is characterised as the active integration and global broadcasting of information, in the form of neural excitation patterns, within a network of "cortical and thalamic areas" (Baars, 2002; Dehaene & Naccache, 2001). The functional cerebral connectivity shown as wMSI excitation in those areas of the brain involved in cognition at a given time distinguishes between disorders of consciousness such as: "patients in vegetative state (VS), minimally conscious state (MCS), and conscious state (CS)" and the work demonstrates that "distributed ... conscious processing [involves] ... late ignition of fronto-temporal networks, and ... sharing of information in the brain" (King et al., 2013, p. 1914) in the global workspace built on "recurrent loops in posterior networks a distributed ... global workspace or a dynamic core" (2013, p. 1917); this is the correlate of experiential consciousness with enactivity or selective and directed excitatory "recruitment" (excitation of a new area that is drawn into the overall pattern) shown by the late involvement of anterior (frontal and prefrontal) networks, evincing the orchestrating work of the active intellect.

The information sharing detected in these studies is realised by oscillatory resonance between excitation in diverse areas of the brain corresponding to regions of the information space actively being exploited by a human subject at a given time; the enactive and dynamic integration within the network means that any sensori-motor coupling between organism and environment results in selective activation of multiple associations to extract from a given situation the patterns of significance relevant for adaptation—JHJ's "re-re-representation." Brentano's "three beat rhythm" of consciousness (noticing, distinguishing, comparing) also refers to this self-organising activity serving the whole human organism and drawing on a hybrid extensional and discursive environment.

Ellis relates this activity to Sartre's hodological space embedding motivation, active search, and "emotionally interested anticipations" comprising embodied cognition (2010, p. 90) such that the whole pattern of neural activity underpins a sense of what it is like to be someone with a place in and perspective on the world and what is in it:

> [M]idbrain-orchestrated emotional processes are crucial for phenomenal consciousness: frontal areas such as the anterior cingulate must be activated

in order to direct conscious attention and these frontal areas are activated in turn by stimulation of the limbic, thalamic, and midbrain areas associated with transmitting emotional motivations of the whole organism to brain areas that bring the emotions into consciousness and also allow them to direct the processes of attention, imaging, and activation of abstract concepts. (2010, p. 87)

Ellis explicitly invokes Luria's *Working Brain* framework, whereby the brain is always active in human analysis, exploration, and discovery: "[p]erception of objects not only is polyreceptor in character and dependent on the combined working of a group of analysers but also ... always incorporates active motor components" (1973, p. 100). Ellis, like others, possibly underplays the role of speech in this activity, but Luria's explicit focus on speech approaches the active human intellect through shared resources that enable us to navigate a world using diverse "cognitive trails" co-created as products of our second nature and enriching our paths through the world.

## 6    DISTANCING, OBJECTIVISING, THE THIRD THING IN A SPACE OF REASONS

Sartre's hodological map highlights a limitation affecting any human being in coming to grips with the world and its affordances—each of us has limited direct experience and limited techniques of discovery engendered by individual organismic learning history and acquaintance with those states of affairs accessible within a unique cognitive trail. "Propositionising" potentially overcomes this limitation through a normative link between thought (subject to individual cognitive limitations) and truth (objective and common to a maximal set of propositions as shared in the ORN domain of the human cognitive niche). Truth ties what one thinks as an individual to facts (situations as propositionalised and subject to the normative influences of objectivity, reason, and reflection). Language, the currency of communicable meaning, effectively marks the layout of the world as it is for creatures like us. We master that representational system through learning the concepts that internally structure human cognition to become adept at gaining forms of knowledge impossible through individual acquaintance. We are, in fact, immersed in an expanding context of signification (within which items are "held fast" by what lies around them [OC, 152]). Speech therefore enhances acquaintance by combining neural traces: (i) those of causal connection and embodied activity in the world—sensori-motor coupling and (ii) semantic connections constituted by language use. The cognitive grip enabled by these connections (sensori-motor and discursive) incorporates first-person stories of extended sequences of coordinated and informed action in a shared world. Even functions for which we are not (perceptually) well equipped—long-distance navigation, the detection of subvisual or remote objects, or the anticipation of non-obvious contingencies—thereby become part of our circuits of cognition.

### 6.1   Propositionising, Language, and Second Nature: The Norm of Truth and Triangulation

The normativity at the heart of language (and the cognitive processes using "the service of words") pervades what it is like to be conscious in a human way (as Freud understood in distinguishing Id, dominated by affectivity from Ego, operating under the reality principle). Our conscious knowing of the world draws on both, but lives and gives an account of itself according to the norm:

> *Aim at the truth! (You are then equipped to decide whether to speak it and what to do.)*

That cognitive niche favours a self-imposed "second nature" that children instance in their bowel and bladder function (JHJ, 1884, p. 742); here the norms extend the animal proto-imperative "Don't foul the nest and keep yourself clean!" Aiming at truth, in the cognitive sphere, is analogous to what bowel and bladder training is in domestic life—a widespread human imperative roughly captured by: "relate to the world however you need to but master the disciplines and productive techniques of being human around here!" We therefore subject young human beings to "training in Judgment," apprenticing them so that holding of a thing to be true is benchmarked against the possible communicability to another of what one thinks (Kant CPR, B849; Foucault, 2008) that engenders self-*scrutiny* and improvement through reason and argument (Mercier & Sperber, 2011). Thus the norms governing human cognition are seen, inter alia, in the mastery of skills required for communication that will not mislead self or others. Such thoughts feed into our multi-perspectival participation in the ORN world we inhabit (Tomasello, 1999) and allow us to progressively unveil the truth within a diversely experienced but fundamentally shared (objective/maximally intersubjective) world (Davidson, 2001; Gillett, 2008; Husserl, 1954).

Here also "the autonomy of language" emerges from our reconstructing connections and moments of experience by abstraction so that our thought and talk is not immediately evoked by a current situation but introduced into shared situations by our communication. Thus "offline" options and acting on the basis of considered intentions synthesise language, truth, and worldly praxis into a powerful resource by which to rehearse, coordinate, and reflect on our dealings with the world (we have the option of, so to speak, taking a step back, which allows, for instance, metaphor as an enhancement of truth-tracking thought through linking the present moment to a past situation with useful resonances and lessons to be learnt). Metaphors coalesce spaces (in the structure of signification) where our words connect us to the world in different ways (e.g. reading—"try to think what the words are saying!"), or where a different set of connections may come into play (e.g. hunting—"follow that track and see where it leads!" or medicine, where we recast our thinking about disease and immunity using the metaphor of attack and defence). We use metaphors to link one praxis (e.g. of looking for the agent at the centre of a destructive activity) through a symbolic but non-literal echo (micro-organisms are not intentional agents and white cells are not soldiers) to an *imaginary* mode of cognition. Metaphor works because the components of situations with which we are dealing are not just referents "available only to the experiencing organism" as such, but also elements that make sense in different ways. Co-reference and communicability give us access to objects and situations in which diverse and mobile dossiers of information (Evans, 1982) cognitively engage us with them in different ways. Abstract instances of a particular say 'a' arise from a succession of experiences in which it appears and use features common to the way it appears to combine our tracking of it with characterisations (predicative) that tell us what kind of thing is being picked out. The relevant skills require mastery, and are refined by talking about things as part of our shared experience of the world (e.g. "Look at the tidal rip!" "There it is again." "And there.")

## 7    CON-SCIO-US-NESS AND CO-CONSTRUCTING *THE IMAGINARY*

Consciousness engages human beings with the world through sensori-motor coupling as part of their (first nature or) natural human constitution (e.g. noticing a disturbance in the water), but enhanced by and through what they have learnt to do with words and the connections inherent in language (a product of second nature). That dual competence makes human cognition and exploring the world a shared venture in which our neural networks are inscribed by discourse, whereby the experience of each can, in a sense, be shared with all. Linguistic sense (*Sinn*) is the key; it "fixes" the meanings of symbols used to co-construct propositions about the world (tied to truth) and generates the human *imaginary*—a set of connected and communicable representations linked at multiple levels:

1. At the level of sensori-motor coupling, we devise techniques to achieve predicted results (What if I comb my fingers through the weeds in my garden in order to pull them out?);
2. at the level of words and concepts, we are alerted to abstract semblances of one reality in another (Is not that pattern, just like the interference of two waves, not a scatter of particles?); and
3. at the level of metaphors, we find ways of dealing with phenomena that otherwise would not occur to us (What if there were illnesses of the mind that came upon a person and rendered them unable to function normally so that they need care and treatment?).

*Con* (With)-*scio* (I know)-*us-ness* (our collectivity)—knowing with others—is a cheap etymological trick but expresses a profound truth. Our brain enacts consciousness as a way of appropriating knowledge gathered both by acquaintance during our cognitive trajectories (or trails) and through shared circuits of adaptive neural integration (Hurley, 2008). Each of us combines that knowledge with the web of cross-connections provided by concepts and argument so as to transform an individual lived world through multi-perspectival communication (Tomasello, 2014). The resulting extensive map of significances, affordances, and opportunities, intersubjectively conveyed, validated, and updated in accordance with norms of communication and truthfulness, is generated within a discursive milieu on the basis of cultural resources. We are therefore creatures whose relationship to the world depends not only on first nature (and its two poles, sensori-motor patterns and external stimulus layouts), but also on second nature coloured, and shaped, by an artful and normative context of embodied and shared life-in-the-world. Our biological potentiality (first nature) inherited from our forebears is therefore transformed by techniques, modes of appreciation, anticipations, and values co-constructed with others to expand our global neurocognitive workspace.

## 8    RECAP ON CHAPTER 3

Hughlings-Jackson's evolutionary neurology links progressively layered sensori-motor function to human social development and propositionising (abstracted from discourse). Thus the informational core of a living soul (realised by human brain function) is "triply indirectly" responsive to the world: (1) through our organismic sensori-motor coupling in which we do and feel things arising in embodied activity, (2) to our inner selves and its natural purposes, and (3) to the lives and worlds of others through language. As a result we ascend levels of adaptation beyond animal capacities to incorporate culture, configuring ourselves to create capacities acquired from our distinctive cognitive niche—the space of reasons and socio-political life. These create an integrated neural network whereby our doings and stories within a cultural setting map the world in shared ways. The two-way dynamic interaction (coupling) of primary experience is thereby elaborated by our being-in-the-world-with-others as we learn "what in social and personal life means something" (Williams, 1985, p. 201). The resulting interconnected neurocognitive structures give us a triple resonance: with consciousness of oneself as an embodied agent, with conversation, and with what we call "conscience"-internalised interpersonal demands (by Jiminy!). That shapes our neural networks into a woven whole vulnerable to a range of dissolutions (in neurological and psychiatric disorders), revealing its composite nature.

### NOTES

1. Hurley (2008).
2. These two phenomena are the principle that "neurons that fire together wire together" (Spitzer, 1999, pp. 40–42) and the idea that a connection followed by a reinforcement will persist (Dennett, 1978, p. 71ff), respectively.
3. Hannah Arendt's complaint against Eichmann "*nicht denken*" was that he had done what he had done without properly taking note of what he was dealing with—the lives of Jewish men, women, and children.

4. These are not the same, but the theory that Van Fraasen enunciates in *Scientific Representation* has a great deal in common with post-structuralism and the layers of interconnected meanings there.

## REFERENCES AND BIBLIOGRAPHY

Baars, B. (2002). The conscious access hypothesis: Origins and recent evidence. *Trends in Cognitive Science, 6*(1), 47–52.

Barsalou, L., Brezeal, C., & Smith, L. (2007). Cognition as coordinated non-cognition. *Cognitive Process, 8,* 79–91.

Blackburn, S. (1984). *Spreading the word.* Oxford: Clarendon.

Block, N. (2001). Paradox and cross purposes in recent work on consciousness. *Cognition, 79,* 197–219.

Chemero, A. (2003). An outline of a theory of affordances. *Ecological Psychology, 15*(2), 181–185.

Chemero, A. (2009). *Radical embodied cognitive science.* Cambridge, MA: MIT Press.

Chemero, A. (2011). *Radical embodied cognitive science.* Cambridge, MA: MIT Press.

Chomsky, N. (2006). *Language and mind* (3rd ed.). Cambridge: Cambridge University Press.

Csikszentmihalyi, M. (1990). *Flow: The psychology of optimal experience.* New York: Harper & Row.

Damasio, A. (1996). The somatic marker hypothesis and the possible functions of the prefrontal cortex. *Philosophical Transactions of the Royal Society of London, 351,* 1413–1429.

Davidson, D. (2001). *Subjective, intersubjective, objective.* Oxford: Oxford University Press.

Davis, J., Gillett, G., & Kozma, R. (2016). Brentano on consciousness: A striking correlation with ECOG findings about the cognitive cycle and the emergence of knowledge and meaning. *Mind and Matter, 13*(1), 12–27.

Dehaene, S. (2014). *Consciousness and the brain.* London: Penguin.

Dehaene, S., & Changeux, J. P. (2011). Experimental and theoretical approaches to conscious processing. *Neuron, 70,* 200–227.

Dehaene, S., & Naccache, L. (2001). Towards a cognitive neuroscience of consciousness: Basic evidence and a workspace framework. *Cognition, 79,* 1–37.

Dennett, D. (1978). *Brainstorms.* Cambridge, MA: MIT Press.

Dennett, D. (1991). *Consciousness explained.* London: Penguin.

Dennett, D. (2003). *Freedom evolves.* London: Penguin.

Edelman, G. (1992). *Bright air, brilliant fire: On the matter if the mind.* London: Penguin.

Ellis, R., & Newton, N. (2010). *How the mind uses the brain: To move the body and image the universe.* Chicago: Open Court Publishers.

Evans, G. (1982). *The varieties of reference.* Oxford: Clarendon.

Foucault, M. (2008). *Introduction to Kant's anthropology.* Los Angeles: Semiotexte (FKA).

Franz, E. A., & Gillett, G. (2011). John Hughlings Jackson's evolutionary neurology: A unifying framework for cognitive neuroscience. *Brain, 134,* 3114–3120.

Freeman, W. (1994). Neural networks and chaos. *Journal of Theoretical Biology, 171,* 13–18.

Freeman, W. (2000). A neurobiological interpretation of semiotics: Meaning, representation and intention. *Information Sciences, 124,* 93–102.

Freeman, W. J. (2008). Nonlinear brain dynamics and intention according to Aquinas. *Mind and Matter, 6*(2), 207–234.

Freeman, W. J. (2015). Mechanism and significance of global coherence in scalp EEG. *Current Opinion in Biology, 23,* 199–205.

Friston, K. (2010). The free energy principle: A unified brain theory? *Nature Reviews/Neuroscience, 11,* 127–134.

Gillett, G. (2004). *Bioethics and the clinic: Hippocratic reflections.* Baltimore, MD: Johns Hopkins University Press.

Gillett, G. (2008). *Subjectivity and being somebody: Human identity and neuroethics* (St Andrews Series on Philosophy and Public Affairs). Exeter: Imprint Academic.

Gillett, G., & Franz, L. (2014). Evolutionary neurology, responsive equilibrium, and the moral brain. *Consciousness and Cognition.* Retrieved from http://www.sciencedirect.com/science/article/pii/S105381001400172X

Gillett, G., & Liu, S. (2012). Free will and Necker's cube: Reason, language and top-down control in cognitive neuroscience. *Philosophy, 87*(1), 29–50.

Harre, R., & Gillett, G. (1994). *The discursive mind.* London: Sage.

Hughlings Jackson, J. (1878). On affectations of speech from disease of the brain (1). *Brain, I*(III), 304–330.

Hughlings Jackson, J. (1879). On affectations of speech from disease of the brain (2). *Brain, I*(III), 203–222.

Hughlings Jackson, J. (1884). Croonian lectures on the evolution and dissolution of the nervous system. *Lancet:* (a) March 29, pp. 555–558; (b) April 12, pp. 649–652; and (c) 26, pp. 739–744.

Hughlings Jackson, J. (1887). Remarks on the evolution and dissolution of the nervous system. *British Journal of Psychiatry, 33,* 25–48.

Hurford, J. R. (2003). The neural basis of predicate-argument structure. *Behavioral and Brain Sciences, 26,* 261–316.

Hurley, S. (2008). The shared circuits model (SCM): How control, mirroring, and simulation can enable imitation, deliberation and mindreading. *Behavioral and Brain Sciences, 31,* 1–58.

Husserl, E. (1954 [1970]). *The crisis of European sciences and transcendental phenomenology* (D. Carr, Trans.). Chicago: Northwestern University Press.

James, W. (1909 [2012]). *A pluralistic universe.* The Floating Press. Retrieved from http://thefloatingpress.com/

Jennett, B., & Plum, F. (1972). Persistent vegetative state after brain damage. *The Lancet, 1,* 734–737.

Kim, J. (2010). *Essays in the metaphysics of mind.* Oxford: Oxford University Press.

King, J. R., Sitt, J. D., Faugeras, F., Rohaut, B., El Karoui, I., Cohen, L., et al. (2013). Information sharing in the brain indexes consciousness in noncommunicative patients. *Current Biology, 23,* 1914–1919.

Klimesch, W. (1999). EEG alpha and theta oscillations reflect cognitive and memory performance a review and analysis. *Brain Research Reviews, 29,* 169–195.

Knott, A. (2012). *Sensorimotor cognition and natural language syntax.* Cambridge, MA: MIT Press.

Kolb, B., & Wishaw, I. (1990). *The fundamentals of human neuropsychology.* New York: W.H.Freeman & Co.

Luria, A. R. (1973). *The working brain.* Harmondsworth: Penguin.

McDowell, J. (1994). *Mind and world.* Cambridge, MA: Harvard University Press.

Mercier, H., & Sperber, D. (2011). Why do humans reason? Arguments for an argumentative theory. *Behavioural and Brain Sciences, 34,* 57–111.

Neisser, U. (1976). *Cognition and reality.* San Francisco: Freeman.

Noe, A. (2009). *Out of our heads.* New York: Hill & Wang.

O'Regan, J. K., & Noe, A. (2001). A sensorimotor account of vision and visual consciousness. *Brain and Behavioural Sciences, 24,* 939–973.

Parkin, A. (1996). *Explorations in cognitive neuropsychology.* Oxford: Blackwell.

Pinker, S. (2010). The cognitive niche: Coevolution of intelligence, sociality and language. *Proceedings of the National Academy of Sciences, 107*(s2), 8993–8999.

Rosen, R. (1985). *Anticipatory systems: Philosophical, mathematical, and methodological foundations.* New York: Pergamum.

Sartre, J. P. (1971). *Sketch for a theory of the emotions* (P. Mairet, Trans.). London: Methuen & Co.

Searle, J. (1992). *The rediscovery of the mind.* Cambridge, MA: MIT Press.

Sellars, W. (1997). *Empiricism and the philosophy of mind.* Cambridge, MA: Harvard University Press.

Snowdon, P. (2014). *Persons, animals, ourselves.* Oxford: Oxford University Press.

Spitzer, M. (1999). *The mind within the net.* Cambridge, MA: MIT Press.

Thompson, E., & Varela, F. (2001). Radical embodiment: Neural dynamics and consciousness. *Trends in Cognitive Science, 5*(10), 416–425.

Tomasello, M. (1999). *The cultural origins of human cognition.* Cambridge, MA: Harvard University Press.

Tomasello, M. (2014). *The natural history of human thinking.* Cambridge, MA: Harvard University Press.

Van Orden, G., Pennington, B., & Stone, G. (2001). What do double dissociations prove? *Cognitive Science, 25,* 111–172.

Vygotsky, L. S. (1962 [1929]). *Thought and language* (E. Hanfmann & G. Vakar, Trans.). Cambridge, MA: MIT Press.

Williams, B. (1985). *Ethics and the limits of philosophy.* London: Fontana.

# CHAPTER 4

# Diverse Dissolutions of Consciousness

**Abstract** The dissolution of the highly evolved and complex triply respon-sive and profoundly intersubjective human cognitive system produces neu-rological and psychiatric disorders. The neurological disorders can be identified in terms of sensori-motor functions that have become faulty, but the psychological disorders are more subtle and set us apart from the shared milieu of meaning and relationships that we are adapted to in highly integrated ways not easily analysed in functional or physiological terms. Psychological disorders alienate us from the distinctively human milieu of agreed meanings and shared understanding and therefore go beyond iso-lated sensory or motor breakdowns and concern the higher integrative functions linking our lives together. The resulting conditions—psycho-logical disorders—embed failures, reflecting distinctively human adapta-tion to a shared intersubjective world, and are analysed by "alienists."

**Keywords** Neuropsychology • Consciousness as connectivity • Cognitive access • Embodied cognition

> *Beyond the obvious facts that he has at some time done manual labour,*
> *that he takes snuff, that he is a freemason, that he has been in China,*
> *and that he has done a considerable amount of writing lately I can*
> *deduce nothing else. (p. 17)*

© The Author(s) 2018
G. Gillett, *From Aristotle to Cognitive Neuroscience*,
https://doi.org/10.1007/978-3-319-93635-2_4

Holmes' remarkable feat highlights the way that evolutionary neurology and enactive embodied cognition combine in an understanding of how human beings construct patterns of skilled response involving three types of information: sensori-motor interaction with objects, current interests and purposes, and human discourse. That gives them a reason-responsive grip on a shared world built on intersubjective triangulation and concept use (Kant, CPR B172ff; B848), enhancing our biological fitness through a global neurocognitive workspace (Baars, 2002) shaped around shared circuits of cognitive processing and generating (good-enough) narrative coherence in human stories. But this fragile harmony can break down.

Distinctly human cognitive development adds the influence of a discursive or ORN milieu to our ethological fitness. The result is an interwoven structure of dynamic and evolving cognition that embeds an ongoing process of "representational redescription," which extends Vygotsky's analysis of thought and language (Karmiloff-Smith, 1992) by focusing on "propositionising" as part of human neurocognitive function. The work is done by re-entrant neural interactions between cognitive maps, some of which are derived from our highest level of adaptation (discursive function and its abstractable regularities). This adaptive cognitive framework is central in Lakoff and Johnson's philosophical semantics, and is best characterised as "discursive naturalism" (Harre & Gillett, 1994).

When human discourse is included in the enactive construal of embodied cognition, it facilitates associatively constructed schemata realised by semiotically informed NcAs (Freeman, 2000). Those assemblies are articulated and interconnected as a result of oscillation between dendritic trees/cortical maps, reflected in and contributing to cerebral synchrony. Human ontogeny thus enables a human being to detect markers of significance configured according to a system of concepts actively shaped for the co-creation of cognitive systems fitted (by cognitive apprenticeship) for a world of culture and value (Sterelney, 2013).

The unity of consciousness and its composition (JHJ's "integration" and "coordination") is disrupted by natural and cultural conditions, causing cognitive disconnection and fragmentation. These "natural experiments" serve to underscore the dynamic cognitive unity underlying the human soul and its integrated consciousness, rationality, and self-control.

1   CONSCIOUSNESS, EMBODIED PHENOMENOLOGY,
     AND COGNITIVE INTERACTION

Philosophers discussing consciousness often refer to "zombies"—imagined distant, abstract, and unscary relatives of the zombies of popular fiction with whom they share a lack of spirit. Philosophers' zombies highlight a supposed "gap" between what it feels like to be conscious (P- or Phenomenal—consciousness with P-properties) and the functional or neural interactions constitutive of mental life. Nagel, for instance, explores "what is it like to be a bat," arguing that "the subjective character of experience" (1979) implies that we do not know what it is like to experience the world of bats as they flit around an echo-sensed cave or nightscape. A similar thought inspires "what Mary didn't know" (Jackson, 1986), where "Mary" has comprehensive scientific knowledge about colour vision, but having lived only in a black-and-white environment, she learns something new when, for the first time, she sees a red rose. Intuitively, what she learns from actually seeing the rose is not captured by the science of colour vision; it is what it is like to see something red—a phenomenal fact derived from acquaintance, not from analysis.

Phenomenal (P-)consciousness, on reflection, captures the richness and aesthetic qualities of human experience—features like freshness, being moved in certain ways, and sensing that we are in the presence of a creature to whom life means something. The P-properties of human subjectivity seem other than the causal or mechanistic properties of neural or cognitive function and, for some, that "feeling quality" generates metaphysical intuitions challenging physicalist accounts of our mental life. But do these intuitions provide clear and distinct ideas sufficient for a logical analysis of mind rather than merely indicating a metaphysical malaise needing neurophilosophical "therapy"? Hetero-phenomenological analysis informed by neuroscience and enactivism nudges us towards a deflationary (therapeutic) view.

2   COGNITIVE INTERACTIONS, CONNECTIVITY,
     AND DISCURSIVE BEING: PROBLEMATIC CASES

Some neurological disorders (natural experiments) disrupt our holistic experience of the world and seem to question the idea of the unity of consciousness as the basis of a human soul. Our intuitions about co-consciousness and a single "phenomenal field" (Bayne, 2008) as part of a global workspace view capture the degree to which a human subject is actively working with information in a synthetic way so that the problem of the phenomenal field as distinct from adaptive biological engagement is finessed. Excitation patterns in dynamic neurocognitive maps (and more enduring associative assemblies) built through learning and evincing cerebral synchrony are created by embodied and top-down autopoiesis (Thompson & Varela, 2001). Those dynamic patterns formed during ontogeny (through cognitive apprenticeship) constitute cognitive unity. Thus the Gestalt and integrative effects shaping human perception and cognition (as when I see a red barn) constitute what I perceive as a thing apt to be encountered, rather than a (purely visual) red-barn aspect, a posited two-dimensional sense-datum. Such an ecological theory of the predictive brain supports Bayne's deflationary take on split brain data: "these findings suggest that the availability of content to systems of cognitive consumption in the split-brain is a messy and somewhat fragmented affair, rather than one in which there is a clean division between two clearly demarcated workspaces" (2008, p. 288).

The deflationary view implies that for a subject, S, to be conscious of X is a matter of degree and that neither an apparently sharp intuitive contrast between what is and is not conscious nor the supposedly clear contrast between phenomenal (P) and access (A) consciousness is as it may seem; the apparent metaphysical "bright lines" separating what-it-is-like-to-be conscious (the "subjective character of experience") from ("inferentially promiscuous") accessible (A-)conscious states implicated in cognition and the control of behaviour (Block, 1995, p. 231) fade under a deflationary neurophilosophical analysis.

## 2.1    Neuropsychological Cases

### 2.1.1    The Split Brain
Split brain syndrome, resulting from a commissurotomy or callosotomy, divides the band of fibres connecting the two cerebral hemispheres. A number of such operations were done, and are still being done, to relieve intractable epilepsy arising from one hemisphere (Gazzaniga, 2005). The operation aims to limit the spread of excitation and to prevent the whole brain being recruited in a seizure so that even if the patient still suffers partial seizures, consciousness and a measure of bodily control can, if

possible, be preserved. Given that epilepsy often results from damage to one side of the brain due to trauma or diseases of infancy, one hemisphere is often not functioning well, so there may be no major adverse effects from the disconnection.

In fact, so subtle are the effects of the operation that it was widely believed that "section of the corpus callosum had no adverse effects on behaviour" (Parkin, 1996, p. 111). Most patients, after a recovery period, live untroubled lives and "a typical medical examination would not reveal anything unusual in their behaviour ... their scores on standard tests are normal" (Kolb and Whishaw, 808). But if patients are submitted to tests especially designed to dissect lateralised information processing in the brain (e.g. by specifically directing information into either the left or the right hemisphere), the pick-up and use of information are shown to be more complex than often thought.

Some interpret the findings to indicate that there is not a unity of consciousness in normal human beings, some even speak of one mind in each hemisphere, a spatial analogue of the temporal (night-day) split imagined by Locke (1789, p. 344). Closer examination muddies that picture.

The experimental work uses brief selective presentation of visual stimuli in one or other half of the visual field (Gazzaniga, 1970) to disrupt holistic perceptual performance. Commissurotomy patients' responses are manipulated by selective visual presentation requiring a lateralised response, for example, picking out a presented object to the left with the left hand (both right hemisphere functions), or giving a verbal report (usually a left hemisphere function) of a stimulus on the left (picked up by the right hemisphere). The classic disconnexion syndromes tend to provoke dramatic conclusions: "each hemisphere can ... have its own sensations, thoughts, percepts, and memories ... not accessible to the other" (Kolb & Whishaw, 1990, p. 808).

Disconnection is dramatically exposed by confabulation: if, for instance, a picture of a door is shown "to the left hemisphere" and a different picture—a hammer—"to the right hemisphere" and the patient is asked why the left hand is picking out a nail, the subject may say, "You build doors with nails" (Gardner, 1974, p. 361). The subject here deals with discrepancies and a failure of normal integration by using a technique—confabulation—also seen in amnesic or cognitively impaired subjects. And these problems are not confined to the experimental setting.

"Manual conflict" or "alien hand" is a bizarre condition where one hand interferes with the other: "the patient once grabbed his wife with his left hand and shook her violently while, with his right hand, he sought to rescue her and bring the violent left hand under control" (Gardner, 1974, p. 359). Such observations problematise claims about an essential unity of consciousness (Nagel, 1979; Parfit, 1984; Sperry, 1977). As one watches a patient whose one hand impedes and even actively restrains the other, the profound anomaly is striking.

These data seem to undermine the assumption of the unity of consciousness as, for instance, in Kant's transcendental "unity of apperception" and to support Hume's reductive account of the self as comprising quasi-atomistic moments and contents of human experience from which variable combinations are cobbled together in a contingent, causal-associative way (1740, p. 676).

Kant, however, maintained that human beings are "objects of outer sense" (B415) or "actualities" (B416), as reasoning beings who act coherently and intelligently by integrating their cognitive abilities, memories, and so on to meet the demands of a kingdom of ends. Kant's thought here converges with Wittgenstein's grounding of mental ascriptions, knowledge, and responsibility in our discourse (language games) and our grammatical presence as referents of first-person ascriptions, or Heideggerian "beings-in-the-world-with-others." In each case, an adaptive demand, arising in the ORN domain, motivates an enactive configuration of the global workspace within a context of moral, social, and political life (a community of ends, or purposive rational creatures).

### 2.1.2    Other Neural Disconnection Problems
In various conditions, such as blindsight (and blindsense generally), aphasia, and amnesia, the functions of the brain strikingly lose key aspects of their "messy and somewhat fragmented" but nevertheless adaptive and effective integration.

These cognitive disconnection syndromes (breakdowns of cerebral synchrony) were originally described by Weiskrantz (and others) in the 1970s and 1980s:

[I]n every area of cognitive neuropsychology there are preserved capacities of which the patients remain unaware. These range from perception to attention, meaning, long term memory, and language, and within each of these categories there are several different varieties. The blindsight patient can discriminate visual stimuli without seeing the stimuli; the blindtouch ("numbsense") patient can locate the position of a tactile stimulus on the arm which has lost its sense of touch. The amnesic patient can store information that can be retrieved by the experimenter but is not acknowledged as a memory by the patient. In prosopagnosia there is a loss of specific memories of familiar faces but the patient demonstrates through indirect means that this information is retained. In unilateral neglect, information can still be processed in the left side of visual space even though the patient not only denies seeing it, but behaviourally ignores it. And a patient who has lost the ability to comprehend language can nevertheless demonstrate through 'on-line' reaction time testing that there is an intact capacity to process both semantic and syntactic information, of which the subject remains ignorant and which cannot be used in his or her discourse. (1997, p. 228)

Amnesia and aphasia each produce cognitive discontinuities contrasting with the underlying holism of function in an engaged human subject who picks up the significance or meaning unifying their lived experience even if they cannot make it explicit, as seen in an anecdote about a patient with amnesia:

The anecdote … describes the amnesic subject whose hand was stuck with a pin by Claparede during an examination, and who thereafter vigorously withdrew her hand whenever she saw him. On questioning she denied having any idea of why she did so. Claparede persisted relentlessly with his questioning and, eventually, after much pressing, she said, "Well, you never know who might have a pin in his hand." (1997, p. 10)

The patient's remark indicates that diverse memory-related functions (Merleau-Ponty's *traces*) may lurk in less-than-fully-accessible corners of her cognitive workspace. Wittgenstein (PI, e.g. 231e; Z #659ff) gestures at such processes, studied under various names (working memory, short- and long-term memory, episodic memory, source memory, semantic memory, procedural memory). We could say that Claparede's patient has an "alief"—an influential mental state the contents of which may neither be able to access nor rationally reject. The term "alief" names without analysing the problem (Gendler, 2008), an explanation of which rests on the contrast between "action guiding representational states" and the work we do to integrate our neurocognitive states (Hubbs, 2013, p. 605). Claparede's patient shows a defect in declarative knowledge but retention of certain effects of an experience (something like a procedural memory evident in behaviour but not explicitly recalled).

In this and other cases tensions arise in Cartesian intuitions about the human mind: (1) the mind is open to introspection and is transparent to the subject whose mind it is; and (2) our ideas and their contents are co-conscious; what we mean is expressed by the words that we use; any experience and its first-person manifest characteristics causes and explains our reactions and responses to the things forming its contents; and yet (3) even if those links are normally causal and constitutive of mental life, "Gaps" occur in the mind where information plausibly gathered by neurocognitive circuits is not open to the conscious self, a phenomenon also found in psychotic fragmentation of the mind (Stevens & Graham, 2000) to which we come in due course.

Weiskrantz suggests that a commentary is missing, as does Dennett's multiple drafts analysis, both of which put a lot of weight on an articulate narrative output as the core of consciousness. That view implies that pre-verbal events become conscious when we compose a commentary (or narratively capture) them and posits a chain of production going through propositionising to intentional actions and attitudes. It converges with Freud in regarding a consciously lived human story (perhaps offline) as only selectively picking out events in the neuroenvironmental stream and clothing them in discursive form when one learns to tell what has happened to others or oneself. Such a neo-Freudian account (Gillett, 2001a) can, however, be reinterpreted as the dissolution of connectedness between areas of the brain configured by discursive practices and producing content that can be explored in diverse ways to engender conscious awareness through selective "synchronising" of excitation in the global cognitive workspace. On the latter interpretation, being conscious is using one's cerebro-somatic connectedness to "fill in" the aspectual shape of perception, cognition, imagination, reasoning, intention, action, or communication. In that way the intentional structure of human thought and action (Gillett, 2001b; Vallacher & Wegner, 1985) reflects "the service of words" (JHJ) and is enactively articulated through representational redescription of one's subjective trajectory through the world even if the form of the cognitive stream is more or less telegraphic and "mental acts" unfold as best they can (in the light of available information) to capture what is significant to a subject.

*Prosopagnosia, blindsight, and so on.* Prosopagnosic patients cannot consciously identify familiar people but subconsciously react in ways commensurate with their experiences of that person (Bauer, 1984). The same kind of dissociation is found in Capgras syndrome, in which psychotic patients become convinced that a person they know has been replaced by an imposter. Such disconnects resemble that reported by Claparede and patients with blindsight, where the subject is affected by/using emotive or motivational information, of which they claim to be unaware, to adapt to a situation (Weiscrantz, 1997). These phenomena are not explained by P- and A-consciousness; rather the disconnections highlight aspects of neurocognitive activity (viz. emotive resonance, face recognition, visual categorisation, cognitive access, and communicability) that are normally integrated into a seamless whole by well-practised enactive skills operating in the global workspace.

*Subliminal perception.* A person who indicates awareness of something not overtly noticed evinces a neurocognitive engagement insufficiently accessible to appear in a narrative (where one aims at a kind of truth able to withstand scrutiny at the highest level of ORN adaptation). Something similar happens when thinkers access objects through modes of presentation that are de-linked from each other (I might taste Pepsi and like it, but when shown a "Drink Pepsi" slogan, I say, "I hate the stuff.") Therefore "not P-conscious" is best interpreted as "not foregrounded and connected in my workspace by active articulation for my current interest-related self knowledge."

*Background perceptual data.* Block (1995) discusses a conversation in the background of which is a pneumatic drill. At a certain point, he becomes aware of the drill, but, again, rather than A-consciousness without P-consciousness, there is a shift in attentional salience and an active allocation of cognitive resources within the global workspace. Such shifts can be highly counter-intuitive; for instance, some patients with frontal lobe lesions (e.g. created by neurosurgeons as a palliative measure for intractable pain) report that their pain has not changed, but that it no longer worries them. Philosophical questions leap out: *if pain is not troublesome enough to cause any distress, is it really pain?* Or *how can it be the same as the pain that was severe enough to lead a person to have a brain operation to relieve it* (Gillett, 1991)? The neurophilosophy is illuminating. This case and the use of hypnotic analgesia (operating on the frontal circuits connecting pain to motivational mechanisms) do not disclose homunculi or "hidden observers"—Cartesian centres of consciousness fully aware and present throughout the experience—but rather highlight the neural connections underpinning motivational and emotively significant features of pain in embodied critters like us. Those connections feed information into the global workspace so that I alone have my interests and my history and my pain (a grammatical remark), and the connections make it painful, so if it is not painful to me, then a pain-related experience of a very unusual kind is going on. Wittgenstein (PI, #295) uses the term "grammatical" to gesture at the complex human praxis surrounding the term "pain" and the role of self-ascription in that praxis.

*Other examples from perceptual psychology.* Some thinkers analyse cases of poor cognitive access to a stimulus in terms of the mismatch between a stimulus array and a conscious report (e.g. in mutual masking, illusory contours, and stroboscopic illusory motion) and use the mismatch as evidence of P-consciousness without corresponding and congruent access; but the brain dynamically integrates information both from bottom-up and from top-down ("filling in") using contextual and other cues to enactively configure conscious experience (Dennett, 1991; Noe & Thompson, 2004). Thus an assumption that conscious reports transparently represent (or supervene on) lower-order neural states appears to be misinformed (by a passive or bottom-up view of the neurology of human adaptation [Chemero, 2003; JHJ, 1887]). In fact, we actively use cues indicating affordances (loci of biological value) in constructing the interactive neural assemblies underpinning conscious life (with its internal relation to intentional action), and the tapestry of lived experience also reflects the multi-perspectival nature of human discourse (Tomasello, 2014).

*Amnesia.* The A-P binary interprets amnesia as preservation of access without P-conscious memory. But that fails to do justice to the diverse neural connections underpinning experience, for example, "Can the subject use associations enabling correct use of a word or concept?" (semantic memory), "Can the subject reconstruct an experience or answer about it at will?" (recall), "Can the subject specify the exact occasion of forming a memory?" (source memory), and so on. These varieties of access help us understand why, for instance, Anne becomes emotional when her dead husband's name is mentioned, but cannot recall his name when asked. The active resonance in the global workspace connecting declarative memory ("John was my husband.") with emotive traces ("John, a lovely man!") is disrupted for Anne.

Sachs (1985) reports a range of cases in which subjective worlds are fragmented and sometimes rendered incoherent, as in the diary of a patient in whom Korsakoff's psychosis had disrupted many of the dynamic memory links enabling narrative construction:

> His entries remained unconnected and unconnecting and had no power to provide any sense of time or continuity. Moreover they were trivial—'Eggs for breakfast', 'Watched ballgame on TV'—and never touched the depths.

But were there depths in this unmemoried man, depths of an abiding feeling and thinking, or had he been reduced to ... a mere succession of unrelated impressions and events? (p. 34)

Here we see the destructive effect of amnesia on feelings and the inter-connectedness of mental contents comprising "what-it-is-like-to-be"—qualitative features of being human that convey a sense of spirit or depth in a human soul (Kant, A, 124). The internal relations between such aspects of human experience and connectivity are also evident in psycho-pathologies in which we see the discursive or highest level of adaptation prominently involved: depression, psychomotor retardation, or abulia—each arises from "local dissolutions of the highest centres" (JHJ, 1887) integrating emotive-motivational tone into our cognitive life.

## 2.2   Psychiatric Symptomatology

Neuropsychological cases in which diverse information is not dealt with in a characteristically human way demonstrate how the reactions of an intact human organism depend on the seamless holism of perception, cognition, motivation, and a sense of self. Sachs' amnesic patient showed narrative disconnectedness, but Capgras and Cotard delusion (*I am really dead*) both show more circumscribed forms of emotive-descriptive disconnec-tion (Ratcliffe, 2009).[1]

### 2.2.1   Hallucinations

Most hallucinations in psychosis (by contrast with a neurological disorder) appear as voices:

They say all different kinds of things to me. Sometimes nice things, some-times bad things, sometimes just repeating whatever I say. They tell me about other people, before I even meet them. The voices didn't tell me about you. But now they're talking about you and listening. (Jaynes, 1989, p. 160)

Hallucinations are private, often personal and loaded with affect, and inaccessible to others. They are unlike real voices in a conversation and a psychotic patient may be quite specific about that: "the voices come from in my head. Actually from in my right ear." However their connections to other aspects of the situation are often fuzzy "About three weeks ago the voices started and I would look around to see if anyone was there but there never was" (Jaynes, 1989, p. 160). They may be both recognised as distinctive and "felt" differently in terms of self-knowledge and agency: "he could not control these voices and they did not let him control his own mind" (Jaynes, 1989, p. 161).

Current theories of psychosis invoke "breaks" in the synchronous functioning of different cortical and subcortical areas constituting the global workspace (Uhlhaas & Singer, 2006). That workspace allows us to know ourselves, feel at home in the world, and see things as part of a holistic unfolding experience of first-person engagement with a world (an insight that reveals the entanglement of organised human activity and making sense of a shared world). Within the integrated psychosomatic whole that characterises normal human life, hallucinations are quasi-sensory experiences evincing a dissolution of ongoing neurocognitive integration normally mediated by: (1) fronto-temporal synchrony linking together excitation in receptive and psychomotor neural fields (shown by wMSI links between brain areas), and (2) the intersubjective coordination outlined by the shared circuits model of cognition. Together those disruptions result in an *unheimlich*, a highly disturbing phenomenal field—a break in the subject-world relationship affecting thought, intention, and action (Stanghellini, 2004; Sass and Parnas; Svenaeus). Psychotic cognitions, particularly those in which affect is blunted or nullified, result in negative symptoms such as psychomotor retardation and anhedonia. Analysing human actions as produced by integrated processes of motivated information gathering and interpretation implies that "no-win" or systematically ambivalent situations frustrate the perceptuo-cognitive skill development because pay-offs are unpredictable (Bolton & Hill, 1996, p. 314ff), so that Thorndike's law of effect fails to apply.

An enactive global workspace built by cerebral synchrony creates complex skills underpinning self-attribution, thought, conversation, self-perception, and a sense of what is illusory, delusory, or imaginary rather than actual (Hurley, 2008; King et al., 2013; Palvaa, Montoa, Kulashekhara, & Palva, 2010). It therefore yields neurally plausible explanations of both positive and negative psychiatric symptoms.

### 2.2.2    Delusions (e.g. Thought Insertion, Broadcast Thought, Persecution, Misidentification, Distorted Self-knowledge)

Both hallucinations and delusions arise from disruption of the cognitive skills required for experience to be communicable and the subject to converge in judgements and master the (normatively) shaped entours of experience and action in a shared world. Delusions are not just false factual beliefs and abnormal evaluations; they reveal a deep mental disquiet in the subject (Mullen & Gillett, 2014). The "Cartesian" stance—that we have immediate and privileged access to our own mental lives—is undermined by delusions of control, thought insertion, or broadcast thought, which show that a coherent first-person narrative is a complex cognitive attainment requiring cerebral synchrony attuned to our highest level of adaptive self-formation. It therefore reflects a common sense or shared understanding of our lives in the world in terms of "ideas common to all" (Kant, CJ, 117).

Delusions often resemble suspicions and private fancies that common sense actively rejects by using cognitive techniques trained through learning the rule-governed use of concepts. Someone who suffers a mental disorder has, in greater or lesser measure, defects in the validating, balancing, self-reflective skills normally active in perception, concept use, and judgements about experience "in accordance with the collective reason of humankind" (Kant, CJ, 136). These aspects of cognition are vulnerable to "breaks" in neurocognitive functions underpinning second nature and generated by responsive and dynamic neural connectivity (Bolton & Hill, 1996; Gillett, 2008). A human being is therefore deeply threatened by such disruptions to our adaptation to the interpersonal human life-world, so that a person with psychosis suffers alienation or experiential and existential distress of a form often not displayed in standard descriptions of mental disorder.

### 2.2.3 Multiple Personality and Dissociation

Multiple personality disorder (MPD) is based on a psychological turmoil that produces multiple distinct and partly self-contained foci of mental life in a single human individual (Gillett, 2009; Snowdon, 2014). The "personalities" have different names, distinct sets of memories, first-person experiences and character traits, and, in some cases at least, distinct psychometric and physiological profiles (Hacking, 1995) such that there are striking but shifting discontinuities and overlaps between the different named personalities.

Consider the case of Rene (Confer & Ables, 1983), a timid 20-year-old female, prone to guilt, depressed, dependent and retiring, and in a failing second marriage. In childhood she was beaten by both parents, rejected by her mother, raped by her father, and as both parents vented frustrations arising from their own inadequacies, she also watched her siblings being abused. Rene developed five alternative personalities, each with a distinct psychological profile, physiological characteristics and responses, and personal manner: Jeane—a 19-year-old expressive and carefree young woman, self-assured and adventurous; Stella (18yo)—sultry, immature, and promiscuous, with a tendency to ingratiate herself to others (especially Rene's mother); Sissy-Gail (4yo)—often withdrawn and cringing in a thumb-sucking foetal posture; Bobby—a resentful and aggressive teenage boy, protective of his younger brothers, and defiant towards Rene's parents; Mary—deeply religious, forgiving, tolerant, and loving, who prayed for all the family (and the other personalities). Each personality expressed feelings distorted in Rene herself but able, through therapy, to be integrated into a new whole through an understanding of their genesis.

MPD or dissociative identity disorder, along with hysteria, fugues, psychogenic amnesia, and other apparently neurological disorders, has a psychogenic aetiology. None are explained by appeal to P- and A-consciousness; rather they are "state-specific" disconnections in a global workspace, the functioning of which at any time is maintained by enactive processes that express maladaptation to a discursive order, a characterisation obscured by terminology like "multiple incompatible neural state disorder" (Andorfer, 1985; Gillett, 2008).

A neo-Aristostelian account of such disorders examines significant features of ontogeny that go awry in dissociative phenomena, the most studied of which is (hysterical) conversion reaction, where a range of neural anomalies help explain what is seen. Normal subjects show an orienting response to novel stimuli (detected by evoked activity in averaged EEG recordings) that habituates (diminishes) once a stimulus loses its novelty, but of those with a tendency to hysterical disorders, "the majority showed no tendency to habituate" (Meares, Hampshire, Gordon, & Kraiuhin, 1985, p. 261). A personality type prone to develop hysteria was neurally indicated by accentuated late (attention/emotion-related) components in evoked potential studies of the cortex and subcortical structures (Howard & Dorfman, 1986), as shown, for instance, in the auditory evoked potentials of medically unexplained hearing loss (Fukuda et al., 1996).

Human attention systems selectively enhance the excitatory cortical and subcortical connections of signals if they are novel or unfamiliar, and their significance for the organism is unclear. "Hysterical type" individuals therefore cannot achieve the cognitive equilibrium (or cerebral synchrony) needed to register stimulus patterns in a homely, non-threatening, and adaptive way, so they must be highlighted, drawn attention to as a matter of concern. The rest of us enactively fine-tune the affective tone of a manifold in relation to the various cognitive maps in play—prudential, social, and moral (generating good-enough predictions regarding positive and negative contingencies of our responses). The neural attractor states that store these patterns minimise "free energy" (Freeman, 1994; Friston, 2010) by using long latency waves of excitation to harmonise disparate brain areas in encoding techniques that adapt behaviour to the human lifeworld. When these are not well functioning because of a troubled ontogeny, even if they are less fragmented and disorganised than in the chaotic associations of psychosis, personality disorders result.

The hysteric's intense and over-dramatised awareness of affective tone is not clearly and distinctly articulated in detail (Shapiro, 1965), lacks the interpersonal and social skills for well-organised ascending adaptation, and, while engaging and arresting at first, is immature, impressionistic, and unstable, potentiating very defective self-awareness and variably unsustainable reactions to social situations.

Thus a neurophilosophical synthesis analysing the global workspace and its ontogeny elucidates dissociative conditions by dissecting the neural integration of self-monitoring, affectivity, and world-relatedness under the enactive influences shaping the soul and finds there a key to mental disorder.

### 2.2.4   Psychopathy

Psychopaths appear rational and moderately astute about life, human actions, and well-being, but seem quite uncaring about the lives of others. DSM III notes "markedly impaired capacity to sustain lasting, close, warm and responsible relationships with family, friends, or sexual partners," a selective near-blindness to what "in social and personal life counts as something" (Williams, 1985, p. 201). These features are often combined with narcissism, leading to a callous indifference to the effects of one's actions on others, but a clever—manipulative, cynical, and even disdainful—attitude to considerations that may impede one's own immediate or short-term attainment of goals such as "money, sexual opportunities or increased status" (Cornell, Warren, Hawk, & Stafford, 1996). This "dark triad" can cause an imprudent underestimation of the cognitive abilities of others (Paulhus & Williams, 2002) and, along with shortcomings in the cognitive skills constitutive of practical reasoning (Maibom, 2005), make a psychopath neglect dimensions of action and interaction important for long-term sustainability of ordinary ways of being-with-others—"a form of mental derangement" termed "moral insanity" (Augstein, 1996). These defects, however, lead them to underestimate those investigating them.

A person showing both psychopathic behaviour and personality traits (Psychopathy Check List Factors 1 & 2 [Hare & Neumann, 2010]) engages in persistent and recurring violence towards others and also characteristic affective and interpersonal impairments. A malign confluence of biological (including genetic) and socialisation factors "interactively predispose to antisocial behaviour" (Raine, 2002), splitting a child's cognitive development apart from the acquisition of normal human propensities for empathy and sensitivity to the feelings of others, which add moral "colour" to what-it-is-like-to-be a human being.

Psychopathic tendencies to abuse others and disregard their feelings reveal that split at the heart of "second nature" whereby, even if a person knows how things affect other people, such knowledge is used "heartlessly" to manipulate rather than being properly integrated into pro-social action structures. As a result the person's life becomes dominated by self-oriented goals and a restricted horizon of motivations whereby an agent sees others purely as means to certain ends and as lacking intelligence if they sometimes refrain from acts that would be to their short-term advantage.

In psychopathy, the information-guiding skills structuring human interactions tend to lack empathic resonance with others. Thus the top-down effects of human intersubjectivity nurtured through sharing stories, imaginative identification with others, and a tendency to care that potentially makes us finely aware of and richly responsive to others are missing from the cognitive-affective mix.

These various "dissolutions" of evolved cognition, often used to support a distinction between P- and A-properties of human consciousness, all reflect enactive or top-down aspects of human adaptation to a sphere of activity in which holistic, emotive factors shape human behaviour through dealings with others and a heartfelt sensibility to them, even when they are not human. The defects in adapting to such demands (inherent in a shared world) help us to understand the real essence of the human intellect and human consciousness as products of second nature fashioned out of our human biological potential.

## 3 TRIPLY RESPONSIVE NEUROCOGNITIVE ASSEMBLIES

The enactive global workspace theory of second nature and human consciousness focuses on active cognition—a holistic, integrated form of intellectual activity based on brain-world interaction and informed by propsitionising developed through language-related participation in an ORN domain (as in JHJ's evolutionary neurology). Recent embodied cognition (Varela and Thompson, Noe) and global workspace theory (Baars, Dehaene & Naccache, Ellis) often neglects the internal relation between conceptualisation and propositional representation and human communication (Freeman, 2000), but in fact, as noted by Kant and the phenomenologists, these are basic to our ability to tell (in two senses) how things are. Some kinds of access provide reportable, declarative, or surveyable "determinacy of content and vividness of subjective experience" (Morton, 1995) That enable "accessibility of ... information to ... other processes" (Navon, 1995). Thus "two pathways" in the brain deal respectively with spatial and sensori-motor relations to an observer's action space (dorsal) and with intrinsic features of objects (ventral) related to concepts and, for humans, semantic content. The role of language function in the latter ensures communicability and triangulation, both of which, for most of us, are smoothly integrated with embodied interaction and well directed by neurocognitive abilities integrated by the frontal lobes and their mediation of emotive and motivational aspects of experience ("somatic markers"). Those signals that move us may be inarticulate, as, for instance, in our "direct recognitional access" (Tye, 1999) to a familiar face where no individuating description can be given. Even if human cognitive processes widely use "the service of words" (JHJ) or "the participation of speech" (Luria) to add to their richness and potential for connectedness between moments of experience, these are only part of a complex picture ("Only her silently mouthed *Iago*." alerted me to his intentions).

The idea that conscious states (of any type) evince "matched content" or "isomorphism" with a stimulus array and its neural correlates often embeds a bottom-up view of mind and consciousness lying at the heart of most reductive approaches to metaphysics. But such approaches do not account for the data (Dennett, 1991; Noe & Thompson, 2004), and it is plausible that we compose "multiple drafts" of our lives as lived using ecologically honed skills supplemented by rich responsiveness to discourse-based associations and quasi-stable narrative threads in a non-linear tapestry that is our integrated intentional being-in-the-world. Thus our three-way responsiveness—to patterns of sensori-motor coupling, states of the self, and discursive engagement—creates us as hybrid critters who live a nose-quivering, vulnerable, and sensitive life in a world of shocks, surprises, and satisfactions but who are also tuned into a world of imagination, stories, and reason. These together lend a shared palette of colours to our "take" on "what it's all about" and obviate the need for qualia or ineffable aspects of experience to fill out an already complex cognitive picture.

Levine perhaps gives too much away and is too subservient to causal accounts when he remarks:

> I think we are dealing with a distinction between forms of access as well as between phenomenal character and access. One form of access is the sort with which cognitive science deals quite well, the sort that is strictly a matter of information flow, which is itself explicable in terms of causal relations. The other is the sort that is inextricably connected to subjective experience. Although it certainly involves information flow in some way, it involves a whole lot more that we do not remotely yet understand. (1995, p. 261)

He rightly complains that analytical metaphysics stumbles in response to holistic embodied access, but he neglects the way subjectivity and consciousness are dealt with in phenomenology (Zahavi, 2013) and does not consider the human imaginary or the non-linear dynamics of human semiotic immersion as they inform the responsiveness at the heart of our embodied cognition.

Breakdowns of integrated neurocognition can occur through neurological or psychological dysfunction, which produces different profiles in the neurocognitive whole that is the normally functioning human soul. The dissolutions of that integrated function reveal its points of vulnerability which are both neural and psychological and lead to different anomalies which should command philosophically distinct analyses aspects of which take us beyond physicalism into an analysis of complex discursive engagement.

## 4    An Epigenetic Constructivist Conception of Embodied Consciousness

There are many paths to understanding the relation between human consciousness and second nature and they illuminate the five desiderata for a neurophilosophical account of human mental life and the nature of human consciousness:

1. A logically articulate account should yield a clear and distinct idea of how it works,
2. an explanation is required for the evolutionary significance of consciousness,
3. the "reality principle" and the reason-responsiveness of the conscious ego should be displayed,
4. the "critters like us" intuition about the quality of consciousness should be understood, and
5. the link between being conscious in a human-like way and inclusion in our moral community should be displayed.

Embodiment and its implications for the *critters like us* intuition is a good start: all the talk in the world about a brick hitting your foot is not the same as the brick actually hitting your foot. This "bruise factor" is an aspect of embodiment—a causal transaction of a complex flesh-and-blood type connected dynamically with bodily reactions in a totally different way from our response to reports—abstracted descriptions of such events.

Zac, the robot built to explore the habitability of alien environments, can, in his own way, see, hear, smell, sense sharp, hot, cold, firm, rough, and smooth, and produce "Oohs," "Aahs," and "Ouchs." At times Zac may even complain that he feels the creeps (perhaps when his neural network gets a hint of something alarming but is short on detail). We could think, "But Zac is not a critter like us and cannot feel because he is a machine"; that is understandable—certain "quivers and shivers" are so protoplasmic that we cannot imagine them in a "Zac" (it can mechanically fix itself up, for heaven's sake!). Our fleshly vulnerability is so salient in our conscious being that any information processing system—no matter how interested in its own survival—cannot therefore subjectively "live" our (holistic embodied) experience.

Being touched by the world, or reality, sets in motion "a million strings in the cerebral harp" that reverberate throughout our bodies a, felt "chord" of subjectivity not capturable by selecting those aspects of stimulus arrays apt for coded representation and communication. The latter fall so far short of our embodied engagement with the world that "What is it like to be X?" is a bit like "So, in a nutshell, what is it about *Othello* that makes it a great play?"—the poignancy and poetry is in "the whole nine yards" of the thing.

The current account of the soul implicates a range of evolved cognitive skills such as cue detection, pattern recognition, inferential links, and other cognitive tricks constitutive of human engagement in the world.

These alert us to what is significant to subjective embodied creatures able to be touched as we are (Aristotle's *tuche*). Wittgenstein's "we—and our meaning—do not stop anywhere short of the fact" (PI, #95) gestures at this being-touched at the heart of mental life with its many complex meaningful strands.

Consciousness is reliably ascribed to others on the basis of criteria evident in their engagement with their environment as we pick out "truthmakers" for our statements (e.g. "John is conscious.") and propositional attitudes ("Jen is hurting."). These may be difficult to detect, but consciousness, as a neurocognitive state of readiness to intelligently engage with the world, is a feature of others that is intensely interesting to us, so that we search for cues making it manifest (thereby grounding practices of second- and third-person "mind reading"—ascriptions of mental states—in a public world). Because learning to play the language game of mental ascription is a key to our adaptation, we learn to master the internal link between first-person ways of knowing (a distinct perspectival mode of presentation), the states realising that discourse, and the cues telling us what is affecting others so as to ground accessible judgements about their subjective experiences.

Consciousness (intransitive—a global state of awareness) is complex and difficult to summarise, a cognitive state that potentiates and is constituted by many acts of being "conscious of" things (transitive use) forming a world of significance (for action, memory, reason, and emotion—JHJ). Thus consciousness and its intentional—world-involving and purposive—contents are internally linked, the basis of phenomenological analyses of our lives as human souls.

The link to attention illuminates the correct analysis of human consciousness: "the directivity and selectivity of mental processes, the basis on which they are organised, is usually termed attention in psychology" (Luria, 1973, p. 256). Luria's focus on our capacity to cognitively connect with aspects of a situation, to selectively direct our intellectual activity, to abstract and synthesise, is also seen in Brentano's reflection on listening to a musical chord:

> A person who hears a chord and distinguishes every single note that it contains is conscious of the fact that he hears them. But a person who does not distinguish the various notes is only indistinctly conscious of them, since he hears them all together, and is conscious of hearing the whole, which includes hearing every individual note. His consciousness, however, does not distinguish every part of the whole. (1929, p. 25)

Brentano's "clear and distinct idea" of conscious experience encompasses what is variously referred to as the interactive cycle of perception-action (Hurley, 1998), Gestalt figure-ground differentiation (Sekuler & Blake, 1994, p. 144ff), the role of schemata in perception and cognition (Neisser, 1976), and the binding of stimulus properties in manifolds related to actionable objects (Treisman, 1996), all involve the predictive brain constructing the possibilities for ongoing interaction (Friston) and globally using them in adaptation. These neurocognitive processes realise intentionality or (opaque and interested) "aboutness"—the core of consciousness (Gillett & McMillan, 2001). To enact the requisite knowledge, I notice, for instance, a fly on the wall *as something* (a black speck, a piece of dirt, or a fly)—content specifications that depend not only on being coupled with a physical bit of the world (the referent—Frege [1980] or truth-maker—Armstrong [2004]) but also on how I think of it (its cognitive significance—the mental analogue of sense [*Sinn*]—as in Frege and Husserl). The implicit (semantic) abilities deployed here ground propositionising (JHJ), wherein subjects differentiate objects from contexts (as figure from ground) and engage them within cognitive maps of the world used to orient, organise, and plan their activity.

Many animals are conscious in that they direct their activity on the things around them, but despite the flexibility and integration in animal responses not only to particular objects but also to significant aspects of their environment (Gillett, 1992), language and propositionising built on abstract reason-related normativity are not part of the non-human mix. Imagine that Crusoe and a crab, walking along a beach (not together), encounter Friday's footprint; Crusoe thinks <that's a human footprint>. But what of the crab? Is it conscious of the fact that it has crawled across a human footprint? It may make something of lingering olfactory cues, but Crusoe's thought potentiates a complex train of cognitions dependent on conceptions of human beings and their properties, their possible future actions, and the de-centering of his island world, all not dreamt of in the crab's philosophy.

Recall Brentano's three beats: first, the catching of attention; second, binding the stimulus features to "bring forth" a gestalt of an object of experience; third, a wide-ranging set of connections to other thoughts, encounters, and senses/*sinnen*. These "three beats" of human consciousness are applied in perception: (1) in demonstratives which express an ongoing "information link between a subject and an object (Evans, 1982, pp. 145–146)—as in "look at that"—indicating an act of attention to an object noticed but perhaps not characterised; (2) in cognitive abilities characterising the object as a "what"—a meaningful whole bound together as a figure against a ground; and (3) linking the significant object to concepts and conceptions connected to other experiences (thereby unifying different representations in a judgement—Kant [B93]). Representational redescriptions (Karmiloff Smith) show second nature enabling these connections using structures abstracted from speech—that frog, that footprint, that square, that leaf, that chord, that note, and so on, each of which uses a term to render experience as communicable and responsive to reason and critical appraisal by others (Kant, A, 95, 117; Tomasello, 1999, p. 128).

Making links explicit and propositional (or discursive—Kant [B93]) in this way enables reason to work on what is happening "around here right now" at different times and places in a conceptualised world so that conscious experience presents a succession of moments full of linked significance (whether banal or momentous) marking a trajectory through a world at meaningful points. Jamesian "streams of consciousness" portray the sequence of mental operations, many of which direct and focus cognition to items and events in these sequences unique to the subject concerned:

1. Every "state" tends to be part of a personal consciousness.
2. Within each personal consciousness states are always changing.
3. Each personal consciousness is sensibly continuous.
4. It is interested in some parts of its object to the exclusion of others, and welcomes or rejects—chooses from among them, in a word—all the while. (James, 1892 [2011])

James leaves no doubt about the role of shared discursively marked contents: "the race as a whole largely agrees as to what it shall notice and name; and among the noticed parts we select in much the same way for accentuation and preference, or subordination and dislike" (ibid.).

Ali Knott (2012) discusses these explicit episodes generated by active attention and stored as recoverable memory sequences encoding key episodes in our engagement with the world and the objects around us. The linguistic structure and semantic content of sentences and the propositions abstracted from them constitutes semantic abilities that confer a representational capacity able to be elaborated and extended as far as language will go and that is in dynamic non-linear interaction with our being-in-the-world.

There is therefore a continuity between human consciousness and that of our animal cousins, but human thought incorporates the multiplicity inherent in the articulation provided by language (Wittgenstein, 1975, p. #32). That multiplicity is grounded in the use of words and symbols linked to (but detachable from) significant patterns in individual neural networks and to the multi-perspectival register of signification (Locke, 1689, p. 404ff) produced by second nature.

## 5    GETTING IT TOGETHER: SUBJECTIVE BUT INTERNALLY DISCONNECTED BODIES AND NERVOUS SYSTEMS

The human body is autopoietically inscribed by the practices (or disciplines) producing second nature. Active, enactive, and interactive cognitive abilities (subject to discursive norms) create a human form of neurocognitive integration that enables adequate self-presentation in everyday life. McGuigan and his followers (1997) provide persuasive evidence that cognitions are embodied as "covert reactions"—"components of neuromuscular circuits governed by cybernetic principles." Thus "where the striated musculature is totally inactive cognitions are inactive," they are impaired. This radically embodied view analyses all our thinking in terms of covert neuromuscular activity articulating experience partly in response to anticipatory copies of efferent motor patterns or speech acts apt in a given situation. On this view, the brain uses a proprioceptively monitored keyboard (or screen) formed by the body to compose patterns of cognitive activity (rather than just using central processing of "internal" representations). That dynamic brain-body interaction supplements the global workspace and is, to some extent, bilateral, even if the dominant traffic is between one half of the brain and the opposite side of the body. Therefore a split brain patient can use such brain-body dynamic links to re-integrate behaviour (as when we use our faces in the manifest tricks seen in split brain experiments, such as frowning at a wrong answer) and thought (as when we rehearse a cricket stroke or the execution of a telling pass in football). Surviving direct intra-cerebral connections in a "split brain" are therefore only part of the apparatus available for cognitive re-integration in that meaning is (literally) "use" encoded in the many subliminal bodily responses whereby embodied cognition "does its thing."

The emerging picture of psychosomatic holism supplements Dennett's view of conscious life as a selective "take" on the complex neuroenvironmental interaction (coupling) that cobbles together quasi-automatic responses, well-rehearsed strategies, habits, and intentional or voluntary direction using top-down enaction in our global workspace, producing "multiple drafts" (Dennett, 1991) of lived experience. Clark's (2008) cybernetic mind in which representations are seen as coupled interactive routines in dynamic reciprocal bodily connection with an environment is of the same type and also pick up Kant's "natural purposes" (CJ, 217) and Freeman's semiotically informed view of non-linear brain dynamics (2000) portraying the neuroenvironmental stream as combining: (1) covert neuromuscular responses mirroring (*en petit*, as it were) ways of responding to and speaking about things, (2) the role of speech in human consciousness, and (3) the training in judgement that inscribes "second nature" in human beings by configuring their neural networks.

The unity of the intellect is therefore holistic and dynamic, so that to try and find a "self" inside me as a centre (or homuncular locus) of consciousness is futile (as in Hume's empirical introspection and Kant's "paralogisms"). The self as subject of thought and experience (a grammatical referent of self-ascriptions) is an *I think*—an embodied being-among-others with a neurocognitive system shaped by the discursive environment. When the relevant neural connections are disrupted, the whole does its best to perform its role in maintaining the integrity required and to account for what one is doing. Thus human selves—the subjective poles of the acquaintance relations at the root of knowledge (Russell, 1988)—are engaged with an intersubjective world in ways that cannot be reduced to a sum of specifiable physical (or physiological) functions (Freeman, 2008).

Ramachandran (1998, p. 227ff) also espouses a holistic conception of the self and concludes that the self—the private core of the conscious mind—is revealed by the pathologies of self-attribution, to be a social construct. He argues that consciousness integrates embodied, emotive, mnemonic, conceptual, and executive selves, all with different neural bases integrated to form a holistic psyche. His view underscores the grammatical nature of the self, as in Wittgenstein's variety of neo-Aristotelianism, whereby the self is as (discursively) real as a criminal conviction or an *Exit* sign.

## 6    EMBODIED COGNITION AND PROPOSITIONISING

We use the verb "tell" in two quite different ways—"she can tell you herself" and "she can tell that it is a shark." Signs and their senses (Frege and Husserl's *Sinnen*) captured by the meanings of words, each reflect "a complex multidimensional matrix of different cues and connections" (Luria, 1973, p. 306) used to build the stories we indwell. Language, the repository of our cumulative (and shared) human experience, is passed on to our children as a normatively shaped tool articulating and refining a human type of neurocognitive grip on the world so that "voluntary attention is not biological in its origin, but a social act" (Luria, 1973, p. 262). Thus human ethology and enactive work within our neural assemblies adapt us to an ORN context—that of human ethology (Tomasello, 2014). Evans' GC (1982) is a neo-Fregean sketch of conscious thought based on a dynamic repertoire of intentional abilities to represent and appreciate the natures of things. It identifies the neurocognitive trick of selectively binding selective elements of a stimulus array to form a unified NcA drawing on the coupling relation between thinker and world and representations of objects shaped by the demands of unambiguous communication (cf. Kant's "empirical synthesis" and convergence in relation to communicability). Our dossiers of information about an object/referent are supplemented by predicative abilities, a combination that reflects human logic (Hurford, 2003) in ways linked, by reference, and the dorsal (perceptuomotor) pathway to particular objects of acquaintance and, by predication of qualities (through the ventral pathway) each pathway connecting fields forming cognitive maps. The resulting dynamic hyperneuronal assemblies reflect the logical form PREDICATE(x), where the x term rests on tracking an object in egocentric or more general space, and the predicate "is the logical expression of a categorical judgment about some attended-to" (p. 275). Hurford argues that evolutionary pressure towards a PREDICATE(x) structure arises when "the number of possible combinations of predicates and variables exceeded the total number of predicates and variables, counted separately" (p. 282). This bold analysis linking brain structure to philosophical logic attests to the widespread usefulness (in the space of reasons) of object tracking (identification of a referent) and inference based on feature-detecting skills. The predicate logic structure that results generates a map of the world in which states of affairs vary in some respects and remain quasi-stable in others. That type of map attunes human beings to the location of objects and their affordances and the language-enhanced or propositional abilities potentiating communication and the multi-perspectival connectivity of human souls.

Rule-governed and similarity-based recognition are both apt frameworks for the space of reasons and its work. But they are often contrasted in the psychological literature and seem to involve different brain regions.

However, the integration and coordination of responses here outlined implies that they are functionally combined. In an informed post-Kantian analysis different moments of experience can be unified by recognising and abstracting two different types of commonalities: one that picks out and tracks an object, and the other that characterises it. The first is attuned to re-occurrences of the same thing (there is that man again) and is indicated by singular terms. The second trades in general characteristics (which may occur in a unique combination such as "the large blond-haired man that talks loudly and insistently but not always in a well-reasoned way"). Consider the following: (1) *that is a small, green, slimy-looking thing beside a freshwater pool; therefore,* it is a frog; and (2) *frogs are animals, animals require oxygen, so frogs must require oxygen.* All such inferences trade in *Sinnen* and the abilities required to grasp their content. Only one singular term occurs: "that." There are rules for the two types of abstraction, but we often seem to just use associations. The described differences in brain localisation largely follow expected lines based on contrasts between (1) associational integration and (2) step-by-step problem solving according to rules of inference. Both processes use (1) prediction, error detection, pattern matching, and the evolution (e.g. through Kant's training in judgement) of recognitional complexes (evolved neuronal assemblies); and (2) mediated symbolic procedures, a skill-forming part of the common reason of humanity so that our neural evolution evinces the active moulding of cognitive systems by culturally conveyed techniques. Both inform our cognitive maps.

Cognitive maps of many types arise within the active neurocognitive system often focused on different types of processing node: place cells, grid cells, border cells, body position cells, and so on form "interconnected, rapidly changing and tightly coordinated submaps," allowing us to exploit "large pools of stored information" (Derdikman & Moser, 2010, p. 561). Here the physiological is a symbol of the logical (PI, 210e) in relation to which Evans' GC spells out the nature of a propositional structure abstracted from what is shared by all in the space of reasons. Our integrative human cognitive skills use the resources of objective "sense"/*Sinn* to add a richness, depth, and communicability to the referents we encounter, allowing forms of reflection unmatched elsewhere in the animal kingdom (Tomasello, 1999, p. 120ff, 2014).

A subject commanding such abilities, and able to grasp a range of propositions or thoughts about objects and their properties in a relatively unbounded action space, can construct a world of facts (Wittgenstein, TLP, 1.1) and not just respond to presented stimulus patterns. Evans' GC ties our use of information to an articulate intentionality based on contentful, world-directed mental acts produced in and fit for a human domain in which reason has a grip. Thus a question like "What is it like to be a bat" in relation to human conscious experience and the human soul can elicit no succinct answer (because of the "Othello in a nutshell" problem), and the many and varied ways, as conscious subjects, we feel, act on, and interact with things, and investigate, apply concepts, and use our rich repertoire of cognitive abilities to deal with the world at many different levels. "I was not really conscious of it when I first entered the room but something gave me the creeps; then I realised that the thing lying on the floor was a body." Here, the body was present and even (in a sense) noticed, but not *as a body*, even though it gave rise to *the creeps*—an "ur-experience" subsequently morphed by conscious attention into a clear and distinct perception/thought (like Crusoe's "I spied a human footprint!").

We understand our states of mind through a network of meanings with an underlying logical structure: "the idea of a predicate is correlative with that of a (potentially infinite and infinitely varied) range of distinguishable individuals of which the predicate can be significantly, though not necessarily truly, affirmed" (Strawson, 1959, p. 99n). An internal connection between shared terms and intelligibility of cognitive contents enables us to *tell* what is going on and think about it in ways that are clear and distinct in their outlines. The requisite skills are developed and honed to provide a communicable understanding of an intersubjective world. Both singular terms and predicates steer us around that world, linking experiences through what they have in common (either they are of the same thing [that rabbit again] or the same type of thing [red things square things, animate things, thinking things, and so on]). Statements about the soul are the same, so that "I am M" (where M is a mental state) is true when I am in the state we call M around here. Thus "X is/I am conscious" is true when X can be properly attributed the predicate *conscious* on the basis of shared usage. Those judgements delineate publically accessible and communicable X's and attributes of X's (e.g. X attends to certain things, evinces intelligent reactions and responses, and interacts with things in such a way that the use of a global cognitive workspace are manifest [so that rich, even poetic, associations become possible for X]). The necessary interplay of skills such as directed gaze, facial expression, investigative activity, and intelligent response to communication marks the fact that one is conscious of, sensitive to, and able to act on things in distinctly human ways; after all, we can tell such things.

How we do all that in terms of cognitive micro-processing structure is best analysed in terms of links between neuronal group selection, sensori-motor coupling, language, and socialisation? Neural re-entry (or oscillation at selected frequencies) attaches semantic links (from a language-related map) to stimulus patterns responded to in general "banging about" (Edelman, 1992). Socialisation inculcates these competencies so that a human soul learns to recognise, reason about, and remember complex affordances in our shared world and to cognise in human ways (Wittgenstein, 1969, p. #402). Consciousness is therefore evident in each other and communicated about in our everyday dealings with the world (PI, #242). That claim is illustrated repeatedly in clinical life when we rate levels of consciousness by using the Glasgow Coma scale (even though it may take an expert to tell in a difficult case, like LiS). Thus the truth-makers for a claim that X, Y, or Z is conscious are, as Strawson notes they must be, public, normative, and the basis of a discursive practice (not "inner," "Cartesian," or "private" events), even though the epistemic skills used to tell that I, you, or he—X—am/are/is conscious may differ from person to person. Logic, of course, bypasses our fallible ways of telling that things are *thus and so* and concerns what is so.

Children master language in interpersonal interactions (Gallagher, 2005, p. 224; Gillett, 2009, esp., Chap. 8) and so develop the skills required to discern the truths reflecting "a shared engagement in the common world" through "our way of being together and understanding each other" (Zahavi, 2005, p. 165). Our participation in a shared world, scaffolded by words (Vygotsky, 1978), creates social skills enabling self-understanding (Zahavi, 2005, p. 166), resting on complex patterns of interaction that become second nature to human beings. Wittgenstein uses the term "bedrock" to refer to the basic capacities in play and remarks on those foundations:

> Consciousness is as clear in his face and behaviour as it is in myself. (1967, p. #221)
> How do I know this colour is red?—It would be an answer to say: "I have learnt English." (PI, #381)

Does an account of triply responsive NcAs fulfil the desiderata for an understanding of human consciousness and help to resolve the metaphysical puzzles constructed around it? Yes, it does so by locating us in a domain where our highest level of adaptation is to discourse; we tell stories about ourselves and the many diverse aspects of our lives. Those stories create the possibility of appreciating the experiences of another, a communicative responsiveness enabling us to co-construct a world of value in which we learn "what in social and personal life means something." That gives birth both to social consciousness, consciousness of oneself, and indeed to what we call conscience (by Jiminy!)

## 7    RECAP ON CHAPTER 4

The philosophy of the soul can be linked to an approach to neurology dating from the nineteenth century. Problematic cases (natural experiments) reveal fractures in a human being's neurocognitive workspace. They are not best analysed in terms of access (A) and phenomenal (P) consciousness, but are helpfully interpreted as dissolutions of the enactive integrating skills that construct and use a global workspace built from sensori-motor coupling and enhanced by discourse—thinking with, or con-scio-ness. Thus analysed neurocognitive discontinuities serve to illustrate and deepen our understanding of consciousness as the active use of a workspace configured by second nature. As such, consciousness fits us for a co-constructed "space of reasons," an analysis that undermines unrealistic Cartesian (or Cartesian materialist) models of the soul. The neurophilosophy of the human soul therefore begins with embodiment and the skills integrating neural responses in our engaged intersubjective world, where we use symbolic communication to forge a complex engagement that is fragile and subject to both neurological and psychological breaks and strains in such a way to cause the disruptions we classify as clinical disorders.

### NOTE

1. Ratcliffe, M. (2009). Understanding existential changes in psychiatric illness: The indispensability of phenomenology. In M. Broome & L. Bertilotti (Eds.), *Psychiatry as cognitive neuroscience* (pp. 224–244). Oxford: Oxford University Press.

REFERENCES AND BIBLIOGRAPHY

Andorfer, J. C. (1985). Multiple personality in the human information-processor: A case history and theoretical formulation. *Journal of Clinical Psychology, 41*(3), 309–324.

Armstrong, D. (2004). *Truth and truthmakers.* Cambridge: Cambridge University Press.

Augstein, M. (1996). J C Prichard's concept of moral insanity—A medical theory of the corruption of human nature. *Medical History, 40*(3), 311–343.

Baars, B. (2002). The conscious access hypothesis: Origins and recent evidence. *Trends in Cognitive Science, 6*(1), 47–52.

Bauer, R. M. (1984). Autonomic recognition of names and faces in prosopagnosia: A neuropsychological application of the guilty knowledge test. *Neuropsychologia, 22*, 457–469.

Bayne, T. (2008). The phenomenology of agency. *Philosophy Compass, 3*(1), 182–202.

Block, N. (1995). On a confusion about a function of consciousness. *Behavioral and Brain Sciences, 18*, 227–247.

Bolton, D., & Hill, J. (1996). *Mind, meaning and mental disorder.* Oxford: Oxford University Press.

Brentano, F. (1929 [1981]). *Sensory and noetic consciousness* (M. Schattle & L. McAlister, Trans.). London: Routledge and Kegan Paul.

Chemero, A. (2003). An outline of a theory of affordances. *Ecological Psychology, 15*(2), 181–185.

Clark, A. (2008). *Supersizing the mind: Embodiment, action and cognitive extension.* Oxford: Oxford University Press.

Confer, W. N., & Ables, B. S. (1983). *Multiple personality: Aetiology, diagnosis and treatment.* New York: Human Sciences Press.

Cornell, D. G., Warren, J., Hawk, G., & Stafford, E. (1996). Psychopathy in instrumental and reactive violent offenders. *Journal of Consulting and Clinical Psychology, 64*(4), 783–790.

Dennett, D. (1991). *Consciousness explained.* London: Penguin.

Derdikman, D., & Moser, E. (2010). A manifold of spatial maps in the brain. *Trends in Cognitive Science, 14*(12), 561–569.

Edelman, G. (1992). *Bright air, brilliant fire: On the matter if the mind.* London: Penguin.

Evans, G. (1982). *The varieties of reference.* Oxford: Clarendon.

Freeman, W. (1994). Neural networks and chaos. *Journal of Theoretical Biology, 171*, 13–18.

Freeman, W. (2000). A neurobiological interpretation of semiotics: Meaning, representation and intention. *Information Sciences, 124*, 93–102.

Freeman, W. J. (2008). Nonlinear brain dynamics and intention according to Aquinas. *Mind and Matter, 6*(2), 207–234.

Frege, G. (1980). *Translations from the philosophical writings of Gottlob Frege* (P. Geach & M. Black, Eds.). Oxford: Blackwell.

Friston, K. (2010). The free energy principle: A unified brain theory? *Nature Reviews/Neuroscience, 11*, 127–134.

Fukuda, M., Hata, A., et al. (1996). Event-related potential correlates of functional hearing loss; Reduced P3 amplitude with preserved N1 and N2 components in a unilateral case. *Psychiatry and Clinical Neurosciences, 50*(2), 85–87.

Gallagher, S. (2005). *How the body shapes the mind*. Oxford: Oxford University Press.

Gardner, H. (1974). *The shattered mind*. New York: Vintage.

Gazzaniga, M. (1970). *The bisected brain*. New York: Appleton Century Crofts.

Gazzaniga, M. (2005). Forty five years of split brain research and still going strong. *Nature Neuroscience, 4*, 853–869.

Gendler, T. S. (2008). Alief and belief. *The Journal of Philosophy, 105*, 634–663.

Gillett, G. (1991). The neurophilosophy of pain. *Philosophy, 66*, 191–206.

Gillett, G. (1992). *Representation, meaning and thought*. Oxford: Clarendon.

Gillett, G. (2001). Intention and agency. In N. Naffine, R. Owens, & J. Williams (Eds.), *Intention in law and philosophy* (pp. 57–69). Burlington: Ashgate.

Gillett, G. (2001). Signification and the unconscious and "Response to Read". *Philosophical Psychology, 14*(4), 477–498; 515–518.

Gillett, G. (2008). *Subjectivity and being somebody: Human identity and neuroethics* (St Andrews Series on Philosophy and Public Affairs). Exeter: Imprint Academic.

Gillett, G. (2009). *The mind and its discontents* (2nd ed.). Oxford: Oxford University Press.

Gillett, G., & McMillan, J. (2001). *Consciousness and intentionality*. Amsterdam: John Benjamins.

Hacking, I. (1995). *Rewriting the soul*. Princeton, NJ: Princeton University Press.

Hare, R., & Neumann, C. (2010). Psychopathy, assessment and forensic implications. In L. Malatesti & J. McMillan (Eds.), *Responsibility and psychopathy* (pp. 93–124). Oxford: Oxford University Press.

Harre, R., & Gillett, G. (1994). *The discursive mind*. London: Sage.

Howard, J. E., & Dorfman, L. J. (1986). Evoked potentials in hysteria and malingering. *Journal of Clinical Neurophysiology, 3*(1), 39–49.

Hubbs, G. (2013). Alief and explanation. *Metaphilosophy, 44*(5), 604–620.

Hughlings Jackson, J. (1887). Remarks on the evolution and dissolution of the nervous system. *British Journal of Psychiatry, 33*, 25–48.

Hume, D. (1740 [1969]). *A treatise of human nature* (E. Mossner, Ed.). London: Penguin.

Hurford, J. R. (2003). The neural basis of predicate-argument structure. *Behavioral and Brain Sciences, 26*, 261–316.

Hurley, S. (1998). *Consciousness in action*. Cambridge, MA: Harvard University Press.

Hurley, S. (2008). The shared circuits model (SCM): How control, mirroring, and simulation can enable imitation, deliberation and mindreading. *Behavioral and Brain Sciences, 31*, 1–58.

Jackson, F. (1986). What Mary didn't know. *Journal of Philosophy, 83*(5), 291–295.

James, W. (1892 [2011]). The stream of consciousness (First published in *Psychology*, Chapter XI) 1892. Retrieved March 23, 2015, from http://cosmology.com/Consciousness121.html

Jaynes, J. (1989). Verbal hallucinations and precomscious mentality. In M. Spitzer & B. Maher (Eds.), *Philosophy and psycholpathology*. New York: Springer-Verlag.

Karmiloff-Smith, A. (1992). *Beyond modularity*. Cambridge, MA: MIT Press.

King, J. R., Jacobo, D., Faugeras, F., et al. (2013). Information sharing in the brain indexes consciousness in noncommunicative patients. *Current Biology, 23*, 1914–1919.

Knott, A. (2012). *Sensorimotor cognition and natural language syntax*. Cambridge, MA: MIT Press.

Kolb, B., & Wishaw, I. (1990). *The fundamentals of human neuropsychology*. New York: W.H.Freeman & Co.

Levine, J. (1995). Phenomenal access: A moving target. *Behavioral and Brain Sciences, 18*, 261.

Locke, J. (1689 [1975]). *An essay concerning human understanding* (P. Nidditch, Ed.). Oxford: Clarendon, 1975 (hereinafter EHU).

Locke, J. (1789). *An essay concerning human understanding*. Oxford: Oxford University Press.

Luria, A. R. (1973). *The working brain*. Harmondsworth: Penguin.

Maibom, H. (2005). Moral unreason: The case of psychopathy. *Mind and Language, 29*, 237–257.

McGuigan, F. J. (1997). A neuromuscular model of mind with clinical and educational applications. *Journal of Mind and Behavior, 18*(4), 351–370.

Meares, R., Hampshire, R., Gordon, E., & Kraiuhin, C. (1985). Whose hysteria; Briquet's, Janet's or Freud's? *Australian and New Zealand Journal of Psychiatry, 19*, 256–263.

Morton, A. (1995). Phenomenal and attentional consciousness may be inextricable. *Behavioral and Brain Sciences, 18*, 263–264.

Mullen, R., & Gillett, G. (2014). Delusions: A different kind of belief. *Philosophy, Psychiatry & Psychology 23*, 27–38; Delusions and the postures of the mind. *Philosophy, Psychiatry & Psychology 23*, 47–50.

Nagel, T. (1979). *Mortal questions*. Cambridge: Cambridge University Press.

Navon, D. (1995). Consciousness, the local newspaper of the mind. *Behavioral and brain Sciences, 18*, 265.

Neisser, U. (1976). *Cognition and reality*. San Francisco: Freeman.

Noe, A., & Thompson, E. (2004). Are there neural correlates of consciousness? *Journal of Consciousness Studies, 11*, 3–28.

Palvaa, J. M., Montoa, S., Kulashekhara, S., & Palva, S. (2010). Neuronal synchrony reveals working memory and predicts individual memory capacity. *Proceedings of the National Academy of Sciences, 107*, 7580–7585.

Parfit, D. (1984). *Reasons and persons.* Oxford: Clarendon.

Parkin, A. (1996). *Explorations in cognitive neuropsychology.* Oxford: Blackwell.

Paulhus, D., & Williams, K. (2002). The dark triad of personality: Narcissism, Machiavellianism, and psychopathy. *Journal of Research in Personality, 36*, 556–563.

Raine, A. (2002). Biosocial studies of antisocial and violent behavior in children and adults: A review. *Journal of Abnormal Child Psychology, 30*(4), 311–326.

Ratcliffe, M. (2009). Understanding existential changes in psychiatric illness: The indispensability of phenomenology. In M. Broome & L. Bertilotti (Eds.), *Psychiatry as cognitive neuroscience* (pp. 224–244). Oxford: Oxford University Press.

Russell, B. (1988). *On the nature of acquaintance* (pp. 125–174) (reprinted in *Logic and knowledge*). London: Unwin.

Sacks, O. (1985). *The man who mistook his wife for a hat.* London: Duckworth.

Sekuler, R., & Blake, R. (1994). *Perception* (3rd ed.). New York: McGraw-Hill.

Shapiro, D. (1965). *Neurotic styles.* New York: Basic Books.

Snowdon, P. (2014). *Persons, animals, ourselves.* Oxford: Oxford University Press.

Sperry, R. W. (1977). Forebrain commuissurotomy and conscious awareness. *Journal of Medicine and Philosophy, 2*(2), 100–126.

Stanghellini, G. (2004). *Disembodied spirits and deanimated bodies.* Oxford: Oxford University Press.

Stephens, G. L., & Graham, G. (2000). *When self-consciousness breaks.* Cambridge, MA: MIT Press.

Sterelney, K. (2013). *The evolved apprentice: How evolution made human beings unique.* Cambridge, MA: MIT Press.

Strawson, P. (1959). *Individuals.* London: Methuen.

Thompson, E., & Varela, F. (2001). Radical embodiment: Neural dynamics and consciousness. *Trends in Cognitive Science, 5*(10), 416–425.

Tomasello, M. (1999). *The cultural origins of human cognition.* Cambridge, MA: Harvard University Press.

Tomasello, M. (2014). *The natural history of human thinking.* Cambridge, MA: Harvard University Press.

Treisman, A. (1996). The binding problem. *Current Opinion in Neurobiology, 6*, 171–178.

Tye, M. (1999). Phenomenal consciousness: The explanatory gap as a cognitive illusion. *Mind, 108*, 705–726.

Uhlhaas, P., & Singer, W. (2006). Neural synchrony in brain disorders: Relevance for cognitive dysfunctions and psychopathology. *Neuron, 52*, 155–168.

Vallacher, R. R., & Wegner, D. M. (1985). *A theory of action identification.* Hove: Lawrence Ehrlbaum & Associates.

Vygotsky, L. (1978). *Mind in society.* Boston: Harvard University Press.
Weiscrantz, L. (1997). *Consciousness lost and found.* Oxford: Oxford University Press.
Williams, B. (1985). *Ethics and the limits of philosophy.* London: Fontana.
Wittgenstein, L. (1967). *Zettel* (G. E. M. Anscombe, Trans., G. E. M. Anscombe & G. H. von Wright, Eds.). Oxford: Basil Blackwell (hereinafter Z with paragraphs referred to by #nn).
Wittgenstein, L. (1969). *On certainty* (G. E. M. Anscombe & G. H. von Wright, Eds.). New York: Harper
Wittgenstein, L. (1975). *Philosophical remarks* (R. Hargreaves & R. White, Eds.). Oxford: Blackwell.
Zahavi, D. (2005). *Subjectivity and selfhood: Investigating the first person perspective.* Cambridge, MA: MIT Press.
Zahavi, D. (2013) Intentionality and phenomenology: Phenomenological take on the hard problem. *Canadian Journal of Philosophy* 32 (Suppl) 63-92.

# CHAPTER 5

# Consciousness, Value, and Human Nature

**Abstract** Human consciousness emerges from neural evolution as a complex and densely woven whole in which doing and perceiving things and the use of language combine to open up the world for human engagement. That integrated whole can be disrupted by breakdowns in its neurological fabric or in its psychological weaving together through human communication and the shared use of symbols and our relationships with each other. When it functions well, that woven whole engenders certain values—the value of crafted things whose purposefulness can be discerned and contemplated but not fully subsumed by functional considerations and the value of our jointly constructed ethos of mutuality, cooperation, and achievement. Those values respectively inform and emerge from the discourses of art and morality.

**Keywords** Second nature • Value and valuing • Rationality sociality and dependency

> *All over the countryside, away to the rolling hills around Aldershot, the little red and grey roofs of the farm steadings peeped out from amidst the light green of the new foliage.*
> *"Are they not fresh and beautiful?" I cried, with all the enthusiasm of a man fresh from the fogs of Baker-Street.*
> *But Holmes shook his head gravely.*

> *"Do you know, Watson," said he, "that it is one of the curses of a mind*
> *with a turn like mine that I must look at everything with reference to*
> *my own special subject. You look at these scattered houses and you are*
> *impressed by their beauty, I look at them and the only thought which*
> *comes to me is a feeling of their isolation, and of the impunity with*
> *which crime may be committed there."*

Embodied cognition and second nature explicate the thesis that active cognitive skills articulate human consciousness of the world through the integrated exploratory and investigative dispositions of a particular intellect shaped in certain ways. A dynamic sensori-motor "fit" between organism and world evinces the region of the discursive milieu that socialises a human being and informs voluntary action, intentionality, and creativity (McDowell, 1994). Together these unpack an otherwise problematic, although intuitively compelling feature of human life—the creation of value as in the moral and aesthetic worlds, both specialised zones within the space of reasons.

Can the value commitments inherent in our learning to deal well with one another (the basis of virtue) be grounded in an analysis of cerebral connectivity, our enactive configuration, and its development (or distortions thereof)? Arguably it can:

1. As moral agents we are assessed according to the self-control we attain by integrating our actions and attitudes; and
2. as moral patients we are appraised and responded to according to what affects us, how we respond, and the more subtle harms, pleasures and pains than those affecting organisms not party to the complex ends structuring human life.

The human soul erects and uses a system of values, intuitive and schooled, evident in both morality and art. If both ethics and aesthetics rest on our triply responsive neurocognitive assemblies, then reason and sentiment should not be pitted against each other but integrated and coordinated in moral life. A set of goals or value orientations in which passion is used by the active intellect to inform our decision-making is the core of Damsio's somatic marker hypothesis. Aesthetic activity, also evincing top down of conceptual and perceptuo-motor elements and drawing on imagination and cultural or symbolic experience, seems to have a similar structure. That complexity in the human intellect between perceptuo-motor cycles of experience and what moves or fascinates us in a world shared with others of others is evident in metaphor and imaginatively "walking in their shoes."

The richness and aesthetic qualities of the human soul and our moral status as creatures whose mental lives deeply connect us reflect our immersion in a social world and encourage an analysis of value in terms of human intersubjectivity and multi-perspectivality that therefore achieves a reflective and quasi-objective quality (Tomasello, 2014) found in both aesthetics and ethics.

## 1    ECHOES OF HUGHLINGS-JACKSON: LAYERS OF INTEGRATION AND COORDINATION

Moral and social cognition reflect the insight that "humans have a propensity to process information in high-level meaningful units (unified wholes) where possible, reflecting a built-in multi-layer hierarchy of information processing mechanisms" (Franz, 2010, p. 17). Such ascending integrative processes enable "non-automatic" adaptations to complex and ever-changing environments through "re-re-representation" (JHJ). That incremental and ongoing process expands beyond Machiavellian social cognition to a more inclusive plane on which responding to the sensitivities of vulnerable fellow human beings has a special role. By that means, the weakest among us are accorded special regard—a sort of "canary in the mine" status, alerting us to features of our world which may not be salient or evident to reason but have significant implications for us all (Gillett, 2004). Once that becomes part of our cognitive orientation, the sense and sensibilities engendered motivate an attitude of inclusive regard for vulnerable others like us (MacIntyre's *dependent rational animals*).

This evolutionary framework yields empathy and mutual respect as affective-motivational abstractions from embodied cognition and conspecific interactions in-forming human life (Harris, 2003; Mitchell, 2009; Saxe, 2006). Hughlings-Jackson's link between propositionising and the use of language (1879, p. 210) is echoed in Wittgenstein's "the meaning of a word is its use in the language" (PI, #43) and places self-formation in situations where we "do things with words" (Austin) as we situate ourselves among others within a sphere of intersubjectivity (Davidson, 2001; Levinas, 1996). That shared context lets us see that the actions and interests of others mirror our own and are storied in moral terms so that we are subject to "the imperative of the word" (Lacan, 1977, p. 106), the currency of a domain of "oughts."

## 2    ANALYSING MORALITY

The current naturalistic perspective grounds value on social and interpersonal affordances—opportunities for action leading to reward or adverse consequences (Aristotle DA, 427b13–28; Chemero, 2003). Complex possibilities arise because others affect us and coordinated actions and thought multiply our possibilities by creating new opportunities and contingencies:

1. Moral thought is normative, prescriptive, or even imperative, capturing what ought to be done to or by an agent (Hume, 1740; Williams, 1985), often framed in universal, categorical, or absolute (non-negotiable, unconditional) terms. Thus if human beings have a right to life, then one ought to respect that, whoever is in jeopardy or whatever regime they live under (we ought not, for instance, suspend the right because they are Jewish, Gypsy, or Islamic). Universality means that we cannot defuse moral claims because of diverse modes of living or acting.

2. However, moral judgements concern a restricted range of human activity and we can debate whether a phenomenon is a genuine focus for moral concern. For instance, even if one is passionate about rugby or baseball, who wins "the World Series" is not a matter of moral concern (unless questions arise about fairness or some such). Williams' phrase "what in social and personal life means something" (1985, p. 201) captures this restricted focus and the universality of morality applies moral "oughts" just *in virtue of those involved being human*. Morality can therefore be formulated as a set of multiply interwoven rules that shape our neural assemblies to integrate our physical, interpersonal, and symbolic functions with an awareness of what matters to others.

3. Given this sphere of concern, a "cold" use of moral reasoning occurs when we calculate the consequences of an action for those affected but in terms that exclude empathy in favour of rationality, objectivity, or impartiality. A "hot" (or even warm) use re-introduces "sentiments" such as disgust, care, and so on. But the view that reason is the slave of the passions and that moral reasoning is primarily grounded in emotion (Greene & Haidt, 2002) is too quick for several reasons.

First: moral reasoning embodies a range of rules and often requires novel and creative thinking to meet new situations (thus morals and mathematics are both rule governed but can be complex and require considerable creativity). An adequate account of virtue and moral sensibility therefore integrates practical or action-involving skills, motivation and emotion, a propositional cognitive structure, and the dynamism or "spirit" that joins human beings together as a kind of family or community of mutual regard. Kant tellingly speaks of *Geist* (spirit) as "the animating principle in a person" that "must arouse our interest by means of ideas [and] ... sets the imagination in motion" (A 124). This resonates with embodied cognition theory, implying that a cold or austerely rational approach to moral judgement based on a form of problem solving (rather than an incentive or reverence for the good) obscures "the heart of the thing"—an interested regard for others. Thus a combination of "realism and imagination in ethics" (Lovibond, 1983) incorporating a "flow" or joy also evident in creativity brings a sense of life into play that transcends any rational calculus and that grows and is informed as human life becomes more inclusive. Thus a caveman type might know that hitting a woman with a club is not quite the thing, but a SNAG (sensitive new age guy) might also be alert to using "he" or "man" in statements about human beings (a sensibility not dreamt of in caveman philosophy).

Because of the inclusive, nuanced, and polychromatic information to which virtue attunes us, broadly consensual informal rules of conduct governing moral reasoning involve a "reflective equilibrium" (Nussbaum, 1990; Rawls, 1957) that finesses the contrast between sentiment and reason so that "the emotivist dog and its rational tail" (Haidt, 2001), with implicit links to primitive and more highly evolved brain structures, seem naive. JHJ's integrative and inclusive framework and Hurley's shared circuits model cope far better with the subtleties of human life.

### 3   NEUROCOGNITIVE INTEGRATION AND THE MORAL BRAIN

The integration of neurocognitive processes underpinning moral agency and the concept of reflective equilibrium incorporate a nuanced awareness of "what in human social and personal life means something." Rules, habits, complex memories, emotions, reservations/inhibitions, and commitments mediated by general and interpersonal learning, the forging of relationships, and ethical formation (Lovibond, 2002) are all important in this kind of responsiveness and the enacted neural "reservoirs of energy" and "resisting positions" (JHJ, 1887, p. 32) realising it. Those neurally influenced constructs (later to emerge and be elaborated in Freudian theory) implicate limbic circuits and structures, such as the amygdala, paralimbic areas of the cerebral cortex (particularly the right parieto-temporal areas involved in face perception, other recognition, and "people-reading"), and prefrontal executive functions. These areas chart a neural network's receptivity to emotive colour and the reactions evoked in others, often called "mind-reading" (Singer, 2006). The relevant skills feed into the responsive equilibrium that enables us to discern and act well in relation to the values that structure our human world (Gillett & Amos, 2015; Gillett & Franz, 2014).

Human flexibility of imagination and moral thinking (informed by regard for others) is associated with dynamic activity in medial and particularly ventro-medial frontal cortices, bringing together motivation, goal setting, and empathy (Mitchell, 2009). Thus moral thought re-re-represents cognitive routines concerned with human interactions, "mapping" them on to discursively shaped cognitive assemblies and incorporating our attuned responsiveness to others (Singer, 2006), upgrading the "Machiavellian" intelligence found in other primates by including a regard for the most vulnerable—the "canary in the mine" sensibility noted above (Gillett, 2004).

Evolutionary neurology, supplemented by embodied cognition theory and the shared circuits model of behavioural control (Hurley, 2008), generates a mode of agency potentiating moral knowledge and its dynamic flow of thought and action (Gillett & Franz, 2014). The mirror neurone system (MNS), discovered in monkeys as a key mechanism associating motor efferent patterns and the observed movements of others, when linked to a language-based set of capacities in which "words serve us during reasoning" (Jackson, 1884, p. 740) expands moral judgement so that it is both reasoned and reactive (Strawson, 1974). JHJ, Luria (1973, pp. 93–94), and Wittgenstein, all tie propositions to actual human use (1879, p. 210) in a way that grounds the human co-creation of a life-world in which second nature adapts us to an ecological niche of co-constructed value and reasoning (Fullinwinder, 1983, p. 153; Pinker, 2010; Wittgenstein, PI ##224, 241).

Within such a context, one's feelings about oneself and relational connections to significant others, both mediated by limbic and midline structures such as the cingulate gyrus (Northoff & Bermpohl, 2004, pp. 8:102–107) and the insula (Singer, 2006), keep us in touch with our own inner states. These are activated during personalised moral tasks (in which you are "close up to" rather than distanced from what you do) and those dealt with intuitively (2004) or with urgency. Given the role of emotive bonds with significant others in our social worlds, it is not surprising that the fusiform network (in the postero-inferior temporal lobe) used for human face recognition (Kanwisher, McDermott, & Chun, 1997; Ishai, 2008) dynamically connects such emotive activation to a "map" or "catalogue" of faces (inferior temporal gyrus) and human facial expressions (superior temporal sulcus). We, like other animals living in stable groups, thus keep track of others as nodes of reciprocal activity and concern. The resulting "dossiers" of affectively charged information potentiate social cognition and action and the resulting dossiers of information, for human beings, are linked to individual names a discursive key to person-perception and our attitudes to others (these become disordered in Capgras syndrome [Ellis & Lewis, 2001]).

Saxe (2006), analysing distinctly human cognition, notes that, cognitively, human cognition is triadic in its development and therefore partly intersubjective, so that human children incorporate the semantic intentions of others into their lived world (as noted by Kant, Husserl, and Merleau-Ponty). An implicit understanding that others have their own subjective views of the world and that one needs to adjust one's cognitive world to accommodate that reality colours memory, emotion, reasoning, and collaborative action. The self-other-world triad (mediated by the associative hub of the temporo-parietal junction cortex and the MNS in general) plays a central role in the dynamic as a bilateral function with widespread cerebral effects. Attributing explicit beliefs and reasoning ("propositioning") to others perceived as culturally or ethnically similar to oneself is more linguistically mediated (anatomically linked to posterior language areas of the left hemisphere) and contrasts, in terms of functioning brain regions, with the "reading of others" from a seemingly different socio-cultural background, a mode of perception probably built on bodily and affordance-related cues read off from "the common behaviour of humankind ... a frame of reference by means of which we interpret an unknown language" (PI, #206). The right temporo-parietal junction serving the latter is part of a series of cortical associative areas with a significantly different profile from those with (Saxe & Wexler, 2005) dominantly linguistically mediated functions.

The shared circuits of behavioural control coordinate our activity (Hurley, 2008) as beings-in-the-world-with-others and go beyond the sensori-motor skill complexes apt for dealing with objects (the *sensorio-communi* of Aristotle and Kant). They help realise interpersonal skills capturing a sense of our shared life in which perspective taking and recognising the interests of others are both prominent. This complex system seems to be mediated by cingulate and peri-cingulate areas and the ventro-medial orbito-frontal cortices, particularly in the right hemisphere (Lamm, Batson, & Decety, 2007), and supplements cognitive schemata mainly focused on means-ends reasoning mediated by the dorsal prefrontal cortex. Autistic children, whose resonance with and understanding of others is poor, tend to use the latter (impersonal) problem-solving strategies (associated with dorso-lateral frontal areas) in tasks where "reading" others is more usually served by social cognition (Dapretto et al., 2006).

Our ongoing or ascending adaptation to the human world, keyed to the behaviour of others, their intentions, and what they mean to us (Apperly, Samson, & Humphreys, 2005; Mitchell, 2009; Young, Dodell-Feder, & Saxe, 2010), rests on the "core triad" of the theory of mind module—intentionality detection, eye direction discernment, and shared attention (Baron-Cohen, 1995) are linked to the Right Temporo-Parietal Junction (RTPJ), to diverse areas such as the extrastriate body area, the superior temporal sulcus, and the medial prefrontal cortex (Mitchell, 2009; Saxe, 2006). The integrative evolution of intersubjective function (Husserl, Trevarthen, Zahavi) is impaired by the deficient connectivity (via the uncinate fasciculus between the right amygdala and Ventro-Medial PreFrontal Cortex (VMPFC)) in psychopaths (Motzkin, Newman, Kiehl, & Koenigs, 2011), and it shows in their lack of interpersonal connection with others, their deficient impulse inhibition, and their lack of regard for others (all dependent on inhibitory aspects of shared circuits functioning as a key aspect of moral behaviour). The emotive-cognitive play-off they lack is therefore both *reflective* (intra-individual interplay between intuition and principle) and *responsive* (between reactions of self and others), and it underpins normal human "reactive attitudes" (Strawson, 1974). The defects of psychopaths imply that the triadic relations of social cognition can now be analysed as comprising

1. interactions between ourselves and the world;
2. observed exchanges between others and the world, including ourselves; and
3. responses to the orientations and reactions of others (Saxe, 2006).

Reading others by these means, when extended to our most developed level of adaptation, goes beyond "Machiavellian" intelligence (Dunbar & Schulz, 2007) to allow pro-social thought and behaviour generated by "the unifying centres … whereby the organism as a whole is adjusted to the environment," or "the physical basis of the ego" (JHJ, 1887, pp. 34, 35)—the most recently evolved and ongoing "intraneural evolution." That going beyond Machiavellianism potentiates being considerate about what matters to others and moral reasoning (Harris, 2003). That moral colour is able to be enacted in our neurocognitive networks to connect shared subjectivity and volition, and thereby to moderate a left-hemisphere-driven focus on "I" or "me." The more inclusive mode of cognition and action (McGilchrist, 2010) can then be seen as a complex integrative achievement based on ascending neural evolution to cultivate "the better angels of our nature" (Pinker, 2011).

We signal to each other within such an inclusive interpersonal domain about things that *ought* to influence our activity. During psychological development, such communication increasingly affects moral consciousness, social cognition, and executive planning through the medial prefrontal cortex. Here, cognitive aspects of empathy are represented more dorsally (superiorly) and emotional aspects more ventrally (Mitchell, 2009), the latter closely connected to the amygdalo-orbito-frontal circuits (Blair, 2007; Motzkin et al., 2011) enabling "ethical formation" (Lovibond, 2002). The process is strikingly illuminated by JHJ's (1884, p. 742) remarks on "potty training" (also given prominence by Freud), in which children learn to transform a simple visceral function into a socially significant voluntary action through the demands and implicit approvals that shape *second nature* through enculturation (Gillett, 2008).

Second nature includes a number of things—automatised skills, over-practised rituals such as those of dance and etiquette (or good manners), and also deliberative, conscious, and even conflicted moral thinking. "The default process, handling everyday moral judgements in a rapid, easy, and holistic way" (Haidt, 2001, p. 820), though itself complex, is able to be over-ridden when moral judgement "fully integrates reasoning, emotion, intuition, and social influence" (p. 828). When that occurs, to claim that "moral emotions and intuitions drive moral reasoning just as surely as a dog wags its tail" (2001, pp. 828, 830) or that is simplistic. In reality, a fine cognitive balance (whereby our shared dynamic, and responsive activity is coloured by reasoned moral discourse) shapes moral thought and action, and a "growing consensus that moral judgements are based largely in intuition—'gut feelings' … in particular cases" (Greene, 2003, p. 847) is just false.

Dynamic responsivity or sensibility to others rests on detecting and responding to paraverbal and other hints that give away a person's reactions within a conversation. They may be uncomfortable or uncertain but unable to say so. But we are not compelled to respond or to modify our planned course of action. If we do so when we pick up on these subtle realities of the interpersonal, social, and political sphere, we can achieve a kind of *responsive equilibrium* (recalling Hurley's shared circuits model and Rawls' idea of reflective equilibrium) directing moral sense and informing virtue. Unlike purely self-serving cognition, that integrative activity transcends austere reward-and-punishment outcomes designed to achieve individual ends and yields a fine and nuanced awareness of a human situation full of cues and clues about what is going down. Thus, the "caveman type" and a SNAG inhabit different worlds of sense and sensibility in which a complex and dynamic flux of "intuition, reasoning, and social influence interact to produce moral judgment" (Haidt, 2001, p. 829). Interpersonal responsivity of this kind could be called "intuitive," but it is neither unreflective nor merely "gut level" and builds layers of meaning into the "somatic markers" nudging human decision-making (Damasio, 2010). Intuitions are moulded into affects that are discursively saturated by sensitive engagement with others (as, for instance, in the work of Jane Austen) potentiated by the many different ways we use words to do things to each other and enriching experience ("Your letter thrilled me greatly, not least because its words—'noble' and 'caring' sparked in my brain and breast.").

Being able to see the beauty of another and to take joy in relationships, even as we realise that they can wound us (or prick our bubbles) highlights the link between moral and aesthetic sense. Sensibility is to the fore in both spheres and also a cultivated attunement to complex and nuanced areas of thinking where clear messages are not always to be had. Fully explicit guides or actionable policies are not easily formulated in either (some would say not formulable). Ethics or aesthetics therefore take us close to the heart and soul of human life, where cognitive-affective engagements inflect our being. Art exercises us even as it draws us into a flow of experience. Meaningful human relationships cut through the stilted terms in which morality is sometimes framed. If justice is, as Aristotle claims, an extension of friendship and friendship is a kind of love, then morality is about the exquisite connections with others that the various forms of love make available, as, so often, is art. Therefore any investigation of the human soul that neglects love, art, and morality misses a great deal of exactly what it is that makes us human.

## 4    ASCENDING ADAPTATION AND THE MORAL
## AND AESTHETIC BRAIN

JHJ's "higher mental functions" are "continually organising through life" (1884, p. 555): "the climax of nervous evolution … the least organised, the most complex, and the most voluntary" and thereby least straightforward for causal explanation and prediction (unlike primitive reflexes, impulses, and stereotyped reactions). This "ascending adaptation" beyond the simpler demands of life creates learned abilities to inhibit, suppress, and control lower-order patterns by using higher-order intentions to enactively reshape our neural circuits. Human consciousness—an amalgam of "will, memory, reason and emotion" (1884, p. 740)—and autopoietic re-re-representation in complex and nuanced cognitive tasks (such as those involved in moral judgements) potentiates the growth of the soul.

Ascending evolution in the human nervous system (as with "micturition and defecation") marks all civilised behaviour (1884, p. 742) and frontal lobe functions enacting reason-responsive control of behaviour integrate or coordinate neural function, as indicated by Ribot's "le moi est une coordination" (JHJ, 1887, p. 85). The conscious willing self—Kant's *gemut*—is therefore both an abstraction from the active integration of human thought and behaviour (1887, p. 89) rather than a thing (material or immaterial) and its essence as a real presence (*ousia*) among us, as an instance of formed matter with its own internal dynamic and psychophysically integrated constitution (DA, 118; 34). Propositionising (the skill informing belief, imagination, expectations, and complex desires) shapes conscious voluntary activity (1878, p. 312) as a cognitive system using a non-linear dynamic responsiveness in which reality and imagination (offline propositionising) iteratively combine to shape human behaviour and experience.

The coordination of diverse cognitive processes in moral thinking and aesthetic life plausibly ascends from mind-reading and skilled invention to enter into a dynamic self-other exchange. Moral action, like intelligent conversation, requires "precise adaptation to new and special circumstances" (JHJ, 1879, p. 219), within the compass of life and potentially beyond it. Neither "cold" impartial calculations of consequences nor "hot" intuitive personal reactions based on emotion deliver what is needed for either moral or artistic modes of "being-in-the-world-with-others." In each mode, affect programmes (Griffiths, 1997) linked to limbic function are moderated by problem solving, highly developed perception-action schemata, affective receptivity, and responsive intersubjectivity to shape what emerges. Similar complex sensibilities, aspects of second nature, are evident in developed aesthetic experience and in the moral world; in both, stereotypes constantly beckon but should be resisted.

JHJ's complex interplay of "reservoirs of energy" and "resisting positions" evident in human neural evolution (1887, p. 32) comprises emotional sensitivity, imagination, strategic thinking, and self-control, allowing selective activation and inhibition attuning us to a shared form of life. Integration between prediction, anticipation, action-planning, and creativity emerges within that holistic context and expands our consciousness. Morality and artistic engagement call us beyond egocentric biological interests and reflect our entanglement with each other, an order of things in which virtue, the ability to share imaginative creations, and moral perception arise. Evolved neural networks at that level intuitively grasp human situations, "the lines along which they are connected and engender one another" (Foucault, 1984, p. 56), and enable a mode of cognitive integration proper to *the true and the good*, a type of being foreshadowed but not realised elsewhere in the animal kingdom. The value discoverable in art and morality therefore gives us the clearest glimpses we have of the true essence of the expanded consciousness that characterises a human soul.

## 5    Recap on Chapter 5: Going Beyond the Self

The human soul is relational, moving through the world in a succession of self-other-world triads that shape an ongoing cognitive evolution evident in many ways, but at the highest level culminating in artistic and moral judgement, their developed sensibilities, and their quasi-objective demands. These form a zone of interaction and competence in the distinctively human world we share and give rise to modes of experience such as love, friendship, and wonder. As such they point to the mystery that is the embodied soul and its open-ended being-in-the-world-with-others.

### References and Bibliography

Apperly, I., Samson, D. E., & Humphreys, G. W. (2005). Domain specificity and theory of mind: Evaluating neuropsychological evidence. *Trends in Cognitive Neuroscience, 9*(12), 572–577.

Baron-Cohen, S. (1995). *Mindblindness.* Cambridge, MA: MIT Press.

Blair, R. J. R. (2007). The amygdala and ventromedial frontal cortex in morality and psychopathy. *Trends in Cognitive Sciences, 13*(9), 387–392.

Chemero, A. (2003). An outline of a theory of affordances. *Ecological Psychology, 15*(2), 181–185.

Damasio, A. (2010). *Self comes to mind.* New York: Random House.

Dapretto, M., Davies, M., et al. (2006). Understanding emotions in others: Mirror neuron dysfunction in children with autism spectrum disorders. *Nature Neuroscience, 9*(1), 28–30.

Davidson, D. (2001). *Subjective, intersubjective, objective.* Oxford: Oxford University Press.

Dunbar, R., & Schulz, S. (2007). Evolution in the social brain. *Science, 317,* 1344–1347.

Ellis, H. D., & Lewis, M. B. (2001). Capgras delusion: A window on face recognition. *Trends in Cognitive Neuroscience, 5*(4), 149–156.

Foucault, M. (1984). *The Foucault reader* (P. Rabinow, Ed.). London: Penguin.

Franz, E. A. (2010). A framework for conceptual binding of bimanual actions: Possible applications to neurology and neuro-rehabilitative therapies. *Current Trends in Neurology, 4,* 1–22.

Fullinwinder, S. (1983). Sigmund Freud, Hughlings Jackson and speech. *Journal of the History of Ideas, 44*(1), 151–158.

Gillett, G. (2004). *Bioethics and the clinic: Hippocratic reflections.* Baltimore, MD: Johns Hopkins University Press.

Gillett, G. (2008). *Subjectivity and being somebody: Human identity and neuroethics* (St Andrews Series on Philosophy and Public Affairs). Exeter: Imprint Academic.

Gillett, G., & Amos C. (2015). The discourse of clinical ethics and the maladies of the soul. In *Oxford handbook of psychiatric ethics* (Vol. I, Chap. 30). Oxford: Oxford University Press.

Gillett, G., & Franz, L. (2014). Evolutionary neurology, responsive equilibrium, and the moral brain. *Consciousness and Cognition.* Retrieved from http://www.sciencedirect.com/science/article/pii/S105381001400172X

Greene, J. (2003). From neural 'is' to moral 'ought': What are the moral implications of neuroscientific moral psychology? *Nature Neuroscience, 4,* 847–850.

Greene, J., & Haidt, J. (2002). How (and where) does moral judgment work? *Trends in Cognitive Neuroscience, 6*(12), 517–523.

Griffiths, P. (1997). *What emotions really are.* Chicago: University of Chicago Press.

Haidt, J. (2001). The emotional dog and its rational tail: A social intuitionist approach to moral judgment. *Psychological Review, 108*(4), 814–834.

Harris, J. C. (2003). Social neuroscience, empathy, brain integration and neurodevelopmental disorders. *Physiology and Behavior, 79,* 525–531.

Hughlings Jackson, J. (1878). On affectations of speech from disease of the brain (1). *Brain, I*(III), 304–330.

Hughlings Jackson, J. (1879). On affectations of speech from disease of the brain (2). *Brain, I*(III), 203–222.

Hughlings Jackson, J. (1884). Croonian lectures on the evolution and dissolution of the nervous system. *Lancet*: (a) March 29, pp. 555–558; (b) April 12, pp. 649–652; and (c) 26, pp. 739–744.

Hughlings Jackson, J. (1887). Remarks on the evolution and dissolution of the nervous system. *British Journal of Psychiatry, 33,* 25–48.

Hume, D. (1740 [1969]). *A treatise of human nature* (E. Mossner, Ed.). London: Penguin.

Hurley, S. (2008). The shared circuits model (SCM): How control, mirroring, and simulation can enable imitation, deliberation and mindreading. *Behavioral and Brain Sciences, 31,* 1–58.

Ishai, A. (2008). Let's face it: It's a cortical network. *Neuroimage, 40,* 415–419.

Kanwisher, N., McDermott, J., & Chun, M. M. (1997). The fusiform face area: A module in Human extrastriate cortex specialized for face perception. *Journal of Neuroscience, 17*(11), 4302–4311.

Lacan, J. (1977). *Ecrits* (A. Sheridan, Trans.). New York: Norton & Co.

Lamm, C., Batson, C. D., & Decety, J. (2007). The neural substrate of human empathy: Effects of perspective taking and cognitive appraisal. *Journal of Cognitive Neuroscience, 19*(1), 42–58.

Levinas, E. (1996). *Basic philosophical writings* (A. Peperzak, S. Critchley, & R. Bernasconi, Eds.). Bloomington: Indiana University Press.

Lovibond, S. (1983). *Realism and imagination in ethics.* Oxford: Blackwell.

Lovibond, S. (2002). *Ethical formation.* Cambridge, MA: Harvard University Press.

Luria, A. R. (1973). *The working brain.* Harmondsworth: Penguin.

McDowell, J. (1994). *Mind and world.* Cambridge, MA: Harvard University Press.

McGilchrist, I. (2010). *The master and his emissary.* New Haven, CT: Yale University Press.

Mitchell, J. P. (2009). Social psychology as a natural kind. *Trends in Cognitive Science, 13*(5), 246–251.

Motzkin, J. C., Newman, J. P., Kiehl, K. A., & Koenigs, M. (2011). Reduced prefrontal connectivity in psychopathy. *Journal of Neuroscience, 31*(4), 17348–17357.

Northoff, G., & Bermpohl, F. (2004). Cortical midline structures and the self. *Trends in Cognitive Neuroscience, 8,* 102–107.

Nussbaum, M. (1990). *Love's knowledge.* Oxford: Oxford University Press.

Pinker, S. (2010). The cognitive niche: Coevolution of intelligence, sociality and language. *Proceedings of the National Academy of Sciences, 107*(s2), 8993–8999.

Pinker, S. (2011). *The better angels of our nature.* New York: Allen Lane.

Rawls, J. (1957). Outline of a decision procedure for ethics. *Philosophical Review, 66,* 177–197.

Saxe, R. (2006). Uniquely human social cognition. *Current Opinion in Neurobiology, 16,* 235–239.

Saxe, R., & Wexler, A. (2005). Making sense of another mind: The role of the right temporo-parietal junction. *Neuropsychologia, 43,* 1391–1399.

Singer, T. (2006). The neuronal basis and ontogeny of empathy and mind reading: Review of literature and implications for future research. *Neuroscience & Biobehavioural Reviews, 30,* 855–862.

Strawson, P. (1974). *Freedom and resentment and other essays.* London: Methuen.

Tomasello, M. (2014). *The natural history of human thinking.* Cambridge, MA: Harvard University Press.

Williams, B. (1985). *Ethics and the limits of philosophy.* London: Fontana.

Young, L., Dodell-Feder, D., & Saxe, R. (2010). Who gets the attention of the temporo-parietal junction? Am fMRI investigation of attention and theory of mind. *Neuropsychologia, 48,* 2658–2664.

# CHAPTER 6

# Second Nature, the Will, and Human Neuroscience

**Abstract** Second nature is what we create in ourselves on the basis of natural capacities comprising first (biological) nature. The self-configuration doing that creative work is an enactive version of what we do all the time. We think of a way things are not but might be (with a little bit of this and a little bit of that) and we make it so. The human will as an origin of what is not but could be brings forth out of thought—the active links we forge between things based on our forms of life—new things. This bringing forth is a creative force in the world that we call the human will. It is always going beyond what is and making what is not (the imaginary) into something real.

**Keywords** The will • Free will and self-formation • Non-linear dynamics • Social discursive and political function

> *Then suddenly another sound became audible—a very gentle soothing sound, like that of a small jet of steam escaping continually from a kettle. The instant that we heard it, Holmes sprang from the bed, struck a match and lashed furiously with his cane at the bell-pull. "You see it, Watson?" he yelled. "You see it?" (p. 111)*

Homes' action becomes intelligible when we realise that the bell-pull is the means of descent into the room for a swamp adder—the speckled

© The Author(s) 2018                                                    123
G. Gillett, *From Aristotle to Cognitive Neuroscience*,
https://doi.org/10.1007/978-3-319-93635-2_6

band—a creature at the centre of a murderous and mysterious set of events. Holmes springs into sudden action as the result of a refined, carefully structured intention evident here in explosive action but elsewhere in more nuanced social interaction. The soul, free will, and voluntary action are knotty areas for definition and diagnosis, and neuroscience is often portrayed as having only a destructive role to play in the metaphysical problem of action and the nosological nightmare created by disorders of volition. In fact, some cognitive neuroscientists argue that our so-called acts of will are really subjective illusions created by self-monitoring of the efferent copies of motor output commands (Haggard, 2008; McGuigan, 1997). Others, however, take a more philosophically robust, Aristotelian stance, whereby the will is our ability to translate reason into action and defects of the will (*akrasia*) are failures in that capacity (Davidson, 1980; Glannon, 2015). Aristotle himself noted that akrasia (incontinence or weakness of the will) was not a problem of movement alone, nor a problem in reasoning, but rather a problem in translation of reason into action. Further reasoning does not solve the problem because it concerns a skill, that of using reason to control action. Aristotle converges with Hughlings-Jackson in highlighting the use of higher levels of "intellect" (or integration) to adapt behaviour to a situation calling for a finely crafted and informed response. This framework illuminates (as outlined above) disorders of volition such as obsessive compulsive disorder (OCD) and psychopathy, two very different breaks of normal and reason-guided conscious self-control (or failures of the will).

## 1    THE DEVELOPMENT OF THE WILL TO POWER

JHJ discusses the will as the highest level of evolved motor control whereby unpredictable and highly divergent factors arising in the human environment are factored into self-direction, making conscious action the least automatic and most highly integrated or coordinated form of behaviour. He noted the complex sources of information in the neural patterns underpinning human behaviour and identified the frontal lobes as the site of active ongoing (we could add socio-cultural) evolution. The coordination and integration of neural assemblies serve the requirements of propositionising as is required in an ORN domain. His holistic theory rejects the posit of a Cartesian mind or centre of consciousness generating impulses that control the motor system about 200 msec before an action occurs (Libet, 1985).

Nietzsche's will to power brings memory, emotion, and reasoning to bear on conscious action, melding emotive and memory-based vectors in the soul. There is a resonance here with the mix between language-related activity (JHJ's propositionising associated prominently with speech centres), ongoing problem-solving strategies (closely related to dorso-lateral frontal areas), and power, "L'effet" (Nietzsche, BGE, 31) organismic efficacy (the motor cortex of the posterior frontal lobe), all part of the brain network subserving voluntary action (Roskies, 2006).

Memory is a catch-all term for a whole series of processes that include learning, source memory, autobiographical memory, and semantic memory, and those neural capacities allow the predictive brain to anticipate and be proactive in such a way as to deal with situations not only according to perceptuo-motor skills personally mastered, but also according to a propositional grasp of pooled human experience and the action structures employed by others and incorporated into one's own multi-layered network of voluntary responding (Wegner, 2002).

Intersubjectivity, emotion, and resonance with others inform the reasoned and conscious control of human behaviour at the highest level, employing strategies of coordination based on neural "centres whereby the organism as a whole is adjusted to the environment" (1887, p. 34). The speckled band is a striking example of the highest level of voluntary integration of perceptuo-motor activity, as Holmes' explosive act is the culmination of an intricate process of reasoning and planning which unravels an apparently impenetrable mystery involving greed, homicide, and human relationships. Holmes weaves his way through the maze of intentions, needs, vulnerabilities, and moral demands to an answer informed by his own, profound but often unrecognised, intersubjective resonance with the protagonists.

Reasoning and its abstract, propositional structure shape volition through the pervasive influence of words and the semantically informed neurocognitive assemblies that underpin our conscious life. The smooth and skilful negotiation of the discursive domain by human beings can lead us to overlook the interwoven nature of deeds, words, and knowledge that forms each of us. But this domain is the locus of the development of the will to power that is the key, for Nietzsche, to psychology. JHJ's thinking in this area not only follows Nietzsche in time and shares his evolutionary orientation, but is, as already noted, remarkably prescient of two great thinkers of the mid-twentieth century—the philosopher Ludwig Wittgenstein and the neuropsychologist Alexandr Luria. The shared and communicable order of thought we use to structure experience locates human action in the "multidimensional matrix of cues and connections" that constitutes word meaning (Luria, 1973, p. 306). That matrix is inscribed in an evolved nervous system imbuing the dynamic which guides human action with a generality and ability to reach beyond the moment to other moments and situations connected by signs and symbols and the concepts linked to them. Thus "[w]ords are required for thinking, for most of our thinking at least but the speechless man is not wordless; there is an automatic or unconscious service of words" (1878, p. 323).

Monkeys mirror the behaviour of other monkeys and perhaps mimic, but the primate MNS circuit is transformed by speech in humans to potentiate our actions and then organise and structure human actions in a domain of reasons, storytelling, and imagination. In fact we often rehearse our moves and postures of the mind "off line" or away from the real-world context of outrageous fortune. Speech, for humans, is not only the currency of social life, but, as Luria and Vygotsky both realised, "a tool for intellectual activity and ... a method of regulating or organizing human mental processes" (1973, p. 307). The skills we master in real discourse and rehearsal enable the optimal use of discursively informed resources grounded in a human, co-constructed ecosphere or cognitive niche.

Through speech we learn both what matters to others and how to "propositionise" knowledge with adaptive value because it allows us to coordinate our behaviour with that of others. Thus power, in the human world, importantly lies in skilful use of words that affect us and inscribe themselves in our souls. Moral consciousness reflects the implicit imperatives of our words because we need to make our way as sustainable organisms in a community of critters like us who make judgements about and interact with each other. Thus JHJ's view of the will—that it coordinates integrated functioning in the most elaborate and least automatic ways—incorporates the uncertainties of the human mode of being-with-others that, at its most developed, is both finely aware and richly responsible (Nussbaum, 1990).

A person who can reason but not translate the results into action suffers from akrasia (Aristotle, NE). Their defect, as noted, is not in reasoning but in a power of an agent which must be learnt and practised. More reasoning is not the answer—execution is what is at stake: "[i]f water makes a man choke, what do you give him to wash it down?" (Aristotle, NE, 1146a 33–35).

Effectively engaging reason with action is a skill which human beings learn. They must also learn judgement, whereby they latch on to the right reasons for the right action at the right time so that they act well. This complex ability is refined by trial and error and the kind of correction that enhances personal efficacy. Defects in this developmental trajectory manifest as poor self-control, for example, outbursts of anger and other such passions which "alter our bodily condition and in some men even produce fits of madness ... incontinent people must be ... in a similar condition to these" (1147a14–18). These manifestations indicate loss of coordination of behaviour by centres that serve the highest levels of integration of activity aided by propositionising or reasoning and they form a kind of (negative) outline of the human will (they show what happens when it is not well functioning).

That lack is seen in OCD, fuelled by anxiety, a pattern of inappropriate, thoughts and/or rituals are evoked by a patient's subjective feelings of threat and insecurity. Freud posited an unconscious mind doing the mischief. In fact, recent neuroscientific research and the use of sophisticated neuroimaging techniques have revealed telling aspects of the neural dynamics and development of such disorders (Whiteside, Port, & Abramovitz, 2004). The limbic and orbito-frontal circuits of behaviour control integrate more emotive or instinctive responses with highly developed problem-solving regions of the frontal lobes (as was discussed briefly in relation to moral thought). Activity in the dorso-lateral frontal areas underpins tasks like reversal learning which indicate flexibility of thinking (Chamberlain et al., 2008). But these areas and the right orbito-frontal cortex show increased metabolic activity, and the left parieto-occipital junction showed decreased metabolic activity in patients, abnormalities positively correlated with the severity of obsessive compulsive symptoms (Kwon et al., 2003, p. 37). We should not draw hasty reductive conclusions here (Whiteside et al., 2004, p. 76) because higher-level integrative functions are non-linearly related to the demands of the complex human ecological niche for which patients are adapted and brain firing patterns are "concomitant," not ultimately causal (Gillett & Harre, 2013).

Two models are often invoked: (1) an executive dysfunction model whereby the patient is thought to have poor impulse control or response inhibition, and (2) a modulatory control model positing that behaviour is ill adjusted to the diverse settings a subject encounters (Friedlander & Desrocher, 2006, p. 34, 40). The evolutionary neurology framework in which selective inhibition and excitation govern oscillatory re-entrant connections between cognitive maps shaped by different contexts suggests that the "reservoirs of energy" and "positions of resistance" in any human being are attuned to demands shaping context-sensitive patterns of response. Impulsive, compulsive, or obsessive behaviour therefore evinces lower levels of integration—(relative) automatism and loss of inclusive information use driven by anxiety, fear, and ill-formed structures of reason-responsiveness.

The dissolution of "moral insanity" (psychopathy) indicates a disconnection of the agent from the moral order such that the "highest motor centres" (prefrontal lobes) or "the physical bases of volition" (1887, pp. 35, 48) does not have the resonance with others that otherwise enhances inhibition and impulse control (Kiehl et al., 2001; Lynam & Gudonis, 2005; Spence, Hunter, & Harpin, 2002) as aspects of second nature. This "local dissolution" (JHJ, 1887, p. 27) spares abilities to pursue pleasure and the know-how to manipulate social situations to achieve it (in the short term). But the result is a degenerate or lesser structure marked by "reduced ... responses to distress cues and threatening stimuli" (Blair, 2003) of central importance in "the painful path to virtue" as a mode of "ethical formation" (Gillett, 2010).

Therefore the thought that the prefrontal areas are the highest centres of motor control "in which evolution is most actively going on" (1887, p. 34) is the dynamic whereby we learn "what in social and personal life means something" (Williams, 1985, p. 201), a type of learning that, in the psychopath's brain, is deficient.

Evolutionary neurology sees the "different insanities" as different kinds of "local dissolutions of the highest centres" of neural function or we could say "disconnects in the soul" that impair new adjustments of the organism, as a whole, to the highly evolved domain of psycho-social adaptation" (JHJ, 1887, p. 34). Disorders of volition show the organism so affected exhibiting poorly moderated behaviours evoked by environmental and internal triggers. More complex lifestyle disorders like addiction reveal a maladaptive fixation of the "appetitive intellect" on some end or zone of activity, for example, a substance and its sub-cultural context.

The present analysis of the will, responsibility, and human freedom sees a human being as adapted to a world of communication and expectations through developing a second or elaborated nature based on the coordination of neural processes that transcend (or are not purely driven by) the biological self and its survival interests to track a shared (and symbolically informed world). The control of behaviour by supra-modal associative networks, such as those of the prefrontal cortex (Mitchell, 2009; Saxe, 2006), uses re-re-representation (through multiple re-entrant cognitive maps), to combine reasoning, argument, and imagination (DA; Gillett, 2008; Mercier & Sperber, 2011); the resulting cognitive assemblies register distress or suffering in others (as detected and mediated within the amygdalo-orbito-frontal circuits, especially those of the right hemisphere), and shape flexibility of responding (as revealed by such things as the Wisconsin card-sorting test and probably mediated by more dorso-lateral frontal areas). The skills of self-integration link our actions to "higher mental processes," embedding other-regarding sensibilities that adapt us to the responses of others and shared symbolic realities of a highly abstract kind.

Human beings function at a psychological level using their neural networks to integrate expectations, imagination, social role conformity, regard for the law, and a myriad other discursive realities (Harre & Gillett, 1994). Non-linear processes shaped within the human ecological niche enable natural processes to emerge, potentiating a form of intersubjective openness to others and responsive self-control (Gillett & Amos, 2015). That self-formation and control are, in part, driven by "the self-images of the age" (as illustrated by the following four cases).

Four Cases: seeing integration and the loss of automaticity in practice.

1. *Irene is distracted by an unexpected movement at the periphery of vision.*

This is an automatic sensori-motor response plausibly arising from a neural process coupling the retina and the oculo-motor systems to serve stimulus tracking, a mechanism showing considerable parity between fairly primitive organisms and human beings, and a lower (physiological) level of dynamic integration where propositionising, reason freedom, and the will do not come into play.

2. *Joe reacts to a perceived personal attack by losing his temper.*

The psychological reaction is at supra-physiological level because Joe's emotive response requires social cognition of some type (and perhaps verbal comprehension). The angry actions exceed Joe's capacity for self-control, even if his reason, to some extent, moderates what he does. This kind of reaction resembles what is seen in akrasia (weakness of the will),

OCD, impulsivity, or emotional incontinence—caused by "inner states" not subject to Joe's conscious will (Glannon, 2015) to a significant degree. He has slipped from the level of neural evolution allowing self-control.

3. *Jason is working towards a high position in his law firm. He goes to the right events and places and, to better himself, divorces his wife, quasi-amicably, to marry the daughter of one of the partners.*

Jason decides consciously, freely, and rationally what to do using a high level of neural integration involving problem solving, social cognition, "Machiavellian intelligence," emotional management, and his ability to negotiate social norms. Second nature is involved and his left-hemisphere-driven, self-oriented processes dominate over his right hemispheric other-related sensibilities. He fashions what some would call "a good life" for himself, all things considered (in a self-serving way).

4. *Kate is married to Leon, her high school "flame." She is a senior liti-gant in a law firm and aiming to be a partner. The senior partner, recently divorced, asks her to assist with a number of his briefs and they often work late together. She ponders the fact that Leon, a professor of philosophy, is no longer the young man she married and has become "less" as she has become "more" in her legal career. She mentions to him, on their way to a performance of The Medea, that their paths seem to be diverging. That night she reflects on commitment, social advantage, ties that bind, and what really matters. On the way home she suggests that they might like to start a family and that, in anticipation, they should talk about their careers and how they would share the load of parenting.*

Note that the third and fourth cases are more detailed than the first two and highlight a contrast between the complex interpersonal world of sec-ond nature and a simpler world approximating the self-orientated ends of first nature (although some animals show "altruism" or self-sacrifice for the group). Cases 3 and 4 raise the issue of rightly ordered appetite, which becomes even more marked if we imagine that Jason learns that his first wife has drifted into alcoholism and a co-habitation relationship in which his two sons are physically abused. He might reflect on his choice—"At the time it was what I wanted but now I realise, as never before, what I have lost and what I have done to others." His freedom to choose and the freedom to act well (to rightly order his appetites under the ideal of The Good) seem to have come apart. His choices could be seen as being made on the basis of alternative values, but some would see a contrast between transient and more enduring values. Such enduring values link us to one another in higher, more demanding ways, through sacrifices and commitments we make and with patterns of human relationship that offset self or personal advantage in favour of other-regarding or even transcendent realities (the kind of thing lauded by major faith traditions). Wolf and other neo-Aristotelians invoke "the True and the Good" in a system of value in which "striking down self-love" (Kant, 1788 [1956], p. 76) may be the path to a "better self." At that level one can ask, "Does second nature allow us to achieve patterns of neurocognitive integration that make us conscious of values that transcend self-oriented needs and advantages?" Many traditions would answer "Yes, and so it should" or even "Yea and Amen!" in the spirit of Wittgenstein's remark "You *ought* to want to behave better" (1965, p. 5).

## 2    RECAP ON CHAPTER 6

Hughlings-Jackson noted, as Kant had before him, that as one ascends from simple linear causal chains in the nervous system to higher and higher levels of integration, one cannot use mechanistic principles to understand what is happening and has to think of the whole organism as cause and effect of certain ways of acting and being. The (non-linear) dynamics that then come into play locate the organism in an environment to which it is adapted. For a human being that environment is discursive, social, and political, and it has complex arrangements that shape his/her participation in ways that are not just emergent from lower levels of engenderment, but act in an autopoietic or top-down manner so that a human being can properly be analysed as a member of the kingdom of ends. That realisation gives meat to the bones of an account of freedom of the will and personal responsibility (especially for the effects of one's actions on others).

### REFERENCES AND BIBLIOGRAPHY

Blair, J. (2003). Neurobiological basis of psychopathy. *British Journal of Psychiatry*, *182*, 5–7.

Chamberlain, S., et al. (2008). Orbitofrontal dysfunction in patients with obsessive compulsive disorder. *Science*, *321*, 421–422.

Davidson, D. (1980). *Essays on actions and events.* Oxford: Clarendon.

Friedlander, L., & Desrocher, M. (2006). Neuroimaging studies of obsessive-compulsive disorder in adults and children. *Clinical Psychology Review, 26,* 32–49.

Gillett, G. (2008). *Subjectivity and being somebody: Human identity and neuroethics* (St Andrews Series on Philosophy and Public Affairs). Exeter: Imprint Academic.

Gillett, G. (2010). Intentional action, moral responsibility and psychopaths. In L. Malatesti & J. McMillan (Eds.), *Responsibility and psychopathy: Interfacing law, ethics, and psychiatry* (pp. 283–298). Oxford: Oxford University Press.

Gillett, G., & Amos C. (2015). The discourse of clinical ethics and the maladies of the soul. In *Oxford handbook of psychiatric ethics* (Vol. I, Chap. 30). Oxford: Oxford University Press.

Gillett, G., & Harre, R. (2013). Discourse and diseases of the psyche. In K. W. M. Fulford et al. (Eds.), *The Oxford handbook of philosophy and psychiatry* (pp. 307–320). Oxford: Oxford University Press.

Glannon, W. (2015). *Free will and the brain.* Cambridge: Cambridge University Press.

Haggard, P. (2008). Human volition: Towards a neuroscience of will. *Nature Reviews Neuroscience, 9,* 934–946.

Harre, R., & Gillett, G. (1994). *The discursive mind.* London: Sage.

Hughlings Jackson, J. (1878). On affectations of speech from disease of the brain (1). *Brain, I*(III), 304–330.

Hughlings Jackson, J. (1887). Remarks on the evolution and dissolution of the nervous system. *British Journal of Psychiatry, 33,* 25–48.

Kant, I. (1788 [1956]). *The critique of practical reason* (L. W. Beck, Trans.). Indianapolis: Bobbs Merrill (hereinafter C PracR).

Kiehl, K., et al. (2001). Limbic abnormalities in affective processing by criminal psychopaths as revealed by functional magnetic resonance imaging. *Biological Psychiatry, 50,* 677–684.

Kwon, J. S., et al. (2003). Neural correlates of clinical symptoms and cognitive dysfunctions in obsessive-compulsive disorder. *Psychiatry Research: Neuroimaging, 122,* 37–47.

Libet, B. (1985). Unconscious cerebral initiative and the role of conscious will in voluntary action. *The Behavioural and Brain Sciences, 8,* 529–566.

Luria, A. R. (1973). *The working brain.* Harmondsworth: Penguin.

Lynam, D., & Gudonis, L. (2005). The development of psychopathy. *Annual Review of Clinical Psychology, 1,* 381–407.

McGuigan, F. J. (1997). A neuromuscular model of mind with clinical and educational applications. *Journal of Mind and Behavior, 18*(4), 351–370.

Mercier, H., & Sperber, D. (2011). Why do humans reason? Arguments for an argumentative theory. *Behavioural and Brain Sciences, 34,* 57–111.

Mitchell, J. P. (2009). Social psychology as a natural kind. *Trends in Cognitive Science, 13*(5), 246–251.

Nussbaum, M. (1990). *Love's knowledge.* Oxford: Oxford University Press.

Roskies, A. (2006). Neuroscientific challenges to free will and responsibility. *Trends in Cognitive Science, 10*(9), 419–423.

Saxe, R. (2006). Uniquely human social cognition. *Current Opinion in Neurobiology, 16,* 235–239.

Spence, S. A., Hunter, M. D., & Harpin, G. (2002). Neuroscience and the will. *Current Opinion in Psychiatry, 15*(5), 519–526.

Wegner, D. (2002). *The illusion of the conscious will.* Cambridge, MA: MIT Press.

Whiteside, S., Port, J., & Abramovitz, J. (2004). A meta-analysis of functional neuroimaging in obsessive-compulsive disorder. *Psychiatry Research: Neuroimaging, 132,* 69–79.

Williams, B. (1985). *Ethics and the limits of philosophy.* London: Fontana.

Wittgenstein, L. (1965). Wittgenstein's lecture on ethics. *Philosophical Review, 74,* 3–26.

# CHAPTER 7

# Consciousness: Metaphysical Speculations and Supposed Distinctions

**Abstract** The human soul and consciousness are active in the world of nature as part of the origins of things and situations informed by human symbolism and propositionising. Therefore the soul introduces human creativity, relationships, reasoning, and imagination into a world of contingency and brute causality, turning it into a partly humanly constructed world. That transformation changes everything through a special kind of non-linearity in which human meanings inflect what happens in our adaptive niche and embeds us in symbolism, culture, and flows of life that transcend causal mechanisms and put human relationships and imagination at the heart of the world shaping us. We therefore become enchanted, storied beings realising forms of life that do not require mystifying varieties of metaphysics to explain their richness.

**Keywords** Consciousness and deflationary metaphysics • Moral being

*"And you, as trained man of science, believe it to be supernatural?"*
*"I do not know what to believe."*
*Holmes shrugged his shoulders.*
*"I have hitherto confined my investigations to this world …"*
*"I see that you have quite gone over to the supernaturalists. But now,*
*Dr Mortimer, tell me this. If you hold these views, why did you come to*
*me at all? You tell me in the same breath that it is quite useless to*
*investigate Sir Charles's death, and that you desire me to do it."*

G. Gillett, *From Aristotle to Cognitive Neuroscience*,
https://doi.org/10.1007/978-3-319-93635-2_7

Holmes proceeds to unpick a seemingly supernatural (or "metaphysical") mystery with analyses and informed insights into human nature, emotions, beliefs, impressions, reasons, observations, and actions familiar from other cases. The mystery ends up being very much of "this world." The metaphysical mysteries of the soul, we might hope, could prove the same. The subjective features of human experience may be able to be made comprehensible and our ideas about them more articulate as a result of Aristotle's approach to human nature. An informed account of evolved human cognitive evolution such as discursive naturalism supplemented by embodied cognition, non-linear, top-down neuro-cognitive processing, and cerebral synchrony seem to illuminate the sometimes elusive realities of human experience and what is meaningful to us. But where does that leave the metaphysics of qualia and so on and so forth?

Human beings are nose-quiveringly alive and tentative prey animals and also formidable predators specialised towards vision and anticipation, based on inclusive information use and ascending re-representation. Our cognitive maps are informed by a sophisticated ORN mode of being and a symbolic order. That extra attunement, and its culturally enriched expansion of the horizons of experience, considerably refines embodied cognition and sensori-motor "coupling" through extensive offline simulation to develop our cognitive powers beyond the limitations of the flesh and our interactive probing and searching of the proximate environment.

Poetics (and art in general) colour our holistic engagement as beings-in-the-world-with-others who must deal with, in Barthes' words, "all the potential of the signified that the poetic sign tries to actualise, in the hope of at last reaching something like the transcendent quality of the thing, its natural (not human) meaning" (1972, p. 133). Art, an adjunct and counterpoint to analysis, uses the play of cognitive faculties to bring a kaleidoscope of imagination and emotion to otherwise everyday functional or linear modes of thought. The resulting inclusive re-creation of moments of experience re-represents the traces of our encounters for contemplation and enjoyment, and animates us in ways connected to acquaintance and its unfailing truth (which Aristotle links to the special senses) but amplified by a richer *aesthesis*.

The human soul distinguishes human beings as an object of special regard in philosophy of mind, epistemology, and ethics, giving rise to three metaphysical speculations:

1. Human consciousness has qualitative properties (*qualia*) making it quite unlike the information processing underpinning cognition in general;
2. human consciousness is normatively informed—moral content and rule-following, each of which determines what we ought to do rather than just describing what we do; and
3. consciousness can focus on non-existent objects of thought and the soul can envisage other (non-actual) worlds.

Can an enactive account of human consciousness do the work needed to clarify these issues?

## 1 ZOMBIES AND QUALIA

Block (and others) argue that Zombies, philosophical creatures with high-level functional access (A-) to neurocognitive information but not phenomenal (P-)consciousness, are entities of which we can form a clear and distinct idea sufficient to ground philosophical analysis of human consciousness. However, given our incomplete knowledge of human neurocognitive function and the complexity of *actual* living systems, thoughts about nominal/apparent and real essence are difficult to get right in relation to human subjectivity (Gillett, 2008; Snowdon, 2014) so that we may not fully grasp the real essence of either the soul or consciousness merely by contemplating introspective phenomena or nominal essences (Kant, CPR, B399ff; Cassam, 1997). Zombies seem to be mechanistic "dry" or "cold" creatures accessing codified information abstracted from real human situations but without the "wet and warm" access we have to emotive and "felt" life as it is lived. When, however, we grasp that the MNS blends observations of the acts of others with the feeling of doing the act oneself, along with links to visceral states, wider sensori-motor associations, and efferent copies of motor patterns (the inner aspect of actually doing things), and with orectic anticipations of reward and satisfaction, the strands of neural excitation informing active cognitive engagement with the world (i.e. *tuche* or acquaintance) look to be rich, complex, and multiply nuanced. Whether any aspects of consciousness are separable from such rich access to our embodied reality is an open question, but given the mismatch between the thought of a bruise on my foot and actually being bruised by a brick hitting my foot, or being gripped by pain and thinking that I am in pain, the embodied view seems to have significant

phenomenological resources inadequately explored in the Zombie literature. Thus Zombies may not, actually, be conceivable and may be a fig-
ment of an impoverished, post-Cartesian philosophical imagination.

Zombies and the A-P distinction have spawned a vast cloud of philosophy, but, as noted, the salient contours of a phenomenon (its "nominal
essence") may mislead us such that only well-informed scientific and conceptual critique displays the "real essence" or *basis in nature* for the referent with which we seem to be acquainted, and when we deepen our
understanding of that, not much may be left over to account for. In fact,
the critics of qualia note the "notoriously elusive" nature of P-consciousness:

> [A] state cannot have a phenomenal property ... unless it is a certain way for
> or to a subject. ... But assuming we have done away with the Cartesian idea
> of an insubstantial or homuncular self, a state can stand in some relation to
> the subject of that state only if it stands in some relation(s) to various other
> states of that subject ... it is plausible to suppose that the relevant relations
> are some sort of access relations. (Church, 1995, pp. 251–252)

This logical problem besets the very idea of the Gap (and the Zombies
that motivate and inhabit it). Embodiment, actual acquaintance, "inferential promiscuity" (Stich), "cerebral fame" (Dennett), or views of consciousness based on embodied integration suggest a "richness of content
and degree of influence" (Morton, 1995)—including emotive and poetic
resonances—that do not seem to neglect anything important in human
experience. "Shall I compare thee to a summer's day" connects "what it is
like to be in love" and "being there" in high summer—a time of enfolding
warmth, fun, light, active bodies, and optimism—rich indeed! Conscious
experience, if the meanings it thrives on do not stop anywhere short of the
fact (Wittgenstein, PI, #95), has these rich phenomenal connections
*through* "abilities to remember and imagine" (Tye, 1999) neurally tied to
moments of direct or indwelt, lived acquaintance.

Frank Jackson's *Mary* (1986) misses out, for instance, on direct recognition—the visual immediacy of colours on a bright summer's day or
being struck by red roses (a colour analogue of *the bruise factor*), a kind of
access that makes the very idea of a Zombie problematic. Imagine Zara, a
child Zombie, at a fair; imagine—she "Ooh"s and "Ahh"s, squeals with
delight, and gives those many little tell-tale signs of surprise, appreciation,
enjoyment, and pain or displeasure shown by human children. Can we
think of her as less than conscious as she responds in such ways? And what
of a Zombie *Byron*, *Shelley*, or *Van Gogh* who engages with our aesthetic

sensibilities? To try and make the Zombie move with any of these cases, to paraphrase Wittgenstein (PI, 420), "does your head in." Is it possible that, as children and poets awaken in us new appreciations and enhance them through exchanges rendering qualitative aspects of the world (the peanut buttery smell of gorse)[1] accessible in new ways, they are not conscious, living souls? Their animation and interest in the world evinces *spirit* (Kant, A 124), and some would say they are cogent counter-examples to the very idea of Zombies (perhaps philosophers' Zombies die the death of a thousand nibbles of properly conceived aesthetic and everyday experience).[2]

The mysteries of consciousness, the soul, and metaphysical appeals to qualia seem to subside in a well-conceived neurocognitive naturalism, but can the enactive theory of our conscious engagement in the real world and a thorough-going exploration of brain connectivity illuminate puzzles that the contested metaphysics aims to address? Due recognition of the richness of discourse and the subtleties of propositionising, it seems to, give us what we are looking for, so that even qualiophiles (like "the new mysterians") and their irresolvable impasses can be offered therapy for the gaps motivating their metaphysical disease.

## 2 "THE GAP" AND THE ENACTIVE REAL ESSENCE OF CONSCIOUSNESS

Having addressed ourselves to the metaphysics of "the Gap" it is worth setting out in detail the answer inherent in a suitable rich Aristotelian response.

1. Wittgenstein treats the gap between brain processes and qualitative aspects of experience by invoking surveyability, the constraints on imagination, the role of imaginability in philosophy (PI, #395), and the problem in knowing or saying that things are thus and so when we try to explicate the semantic relation (Russell's acquaintance) between a (psycho)logical subject and the world (TLP, 4112). A deflationary view emerges from Heidegger's being-in-the-world and his distinction between existence and ideas abstracted from lived moments of *being there* (Clark, 1997).

2. The gap or hard problem submits to an existential-phenomenological reduction, laying bare the elusive nature of the active mind and the value and richness inherent in our human and intersubjective lifeworld. Zahavin's phenomenological analysis of the intentional quality of actively lived experience and enactively constituted mental contents demonstrates such an approach (2013).

3. Locke's *real essences*, as explored in the enactive connectivity model, generate a scientific and neurocognitively informed (hetero-)phenomenology of lived human experience. Human beings are natural beings-in-the-world-with-others acquainted with situations and actively using their rich triply responsive (self-world-discourse) associations and thereby affected both by the cruelty of words and by actual sticks and stones that break our bones (Gillett, 2008, p. 83).

4. The global workspace and its spiralling possibilities prompt a new source of wonder about the intricate neural processes that both couple us to the world and allow us to decouple or go offline to devise, explore, and contemplate elaborate self-understandings that can be inspiring and fill us with wonder (as they did Kant) when he thought of "the starry skies above and the moral law within" (C PracR, 166).

5. We are animated by offline musings to compose propositions about our human embodied experience that potentiate philosophical and poetic understandings of the human condition and its significance in the order of things. These offer us an entrée into the symbolic order.

The appearances through which we construct accounts of our lives form, in effect, nominal essentia abstracted from our lived being that cause some to posit phenomenal (P) and access (A) properties (Block) even if "the best one can do for P-consciousness is in some respects worse than for many other concepts ... all one can do is point to the phenomenon" (1995, p. 230). Such "pointing to" hardly yields clear and distinct ideas that extend the abilities of the predictive brain (in Friston's terms) either in relation to embodied experience or in terms of the articulation of a coherent cognitive map apt to capture the chaotic nose-quivering intimations of being-in-the-world that do not fit into habituated patterns.

Philosophers and scientists explicate what can be objectified or rendered in a way open to established reflection. Both rely on abstractions from our lived experience as embodied agents actually doing things. Abstraction renders being-in-the-world in terms apt for propositions and argumentation, but enactive embodied acquaintance yields "What it is like to be an X" as part of our lived subjectivity—sensations, perceptuo-motor schemata, movements, feelings, excited thoughts, desires, and emotions fill in the apparent "gap" between the holistic richness, wonder, surprise, and ineffability of bodily experience and our intellectual grasp of the austere information yielded by abstraction (Kant, A, 15).

Abstraction, as an active form of access that applies intellectual skills to lived experience as we actively and selectively attend to different possibilities in the global workspace, enables us to think and reason about experience and act upon an interested and selective "take" on embodied *geist*—the shared experience and thought of humanity. That selective "take" generates a narrative comprising derivative cognitive trails variously played piano or forte.

## 3 INTENTIONAL RULE-FOLLOWING

Kant identified conscious rule-following as embodying norms that guide human subjects in their judgements and actions and shape the skills of reason. The component skills required are related to mother wit, something "a lack of which no school can make good" (B172), but are themselves analysable. Aristotle concurs—the inability to apply reason, in thought and action, cannot be displayed or rectified through reasoning— "if water makes a man choke, what can you give him to wash it down?"— what is lacking comes from training and the inculcation of a second nature of the right kind so that one's deliberations are applied to a domain of activity and able to be enacted (NE, 1152a28–30) during self-formation. Thus rule-following is not, or not without distortion, a merely intellectual or functional attribute flowing from encoded rules or propositions forming a kind of calculus (PI, #81), but involves enacting ways of doing things (OC, #402)—the autopoietic ability to bridge the gap between (the propositional structure of) reason and acting, using a technique (whether perceptual or motor) that relates one to the world. That gap, implicit in rule-following, is not a gap in *knowing that* but a gap in *knowing how*, an inflexion of sensori-motor coupling by higher-order neural integration and coordination.

Human beings therefore do not inhabit two worlds or metaphysically distinct "spaces," but negotiate and relate *propositions* and *actuality*, the *abstract* and the *applied, discursive techniques of representation* and *acquaintance, truth-maker* and *truth bearer*. These are not distinct "parts" or domains of reality but distinct ways of conceptualising our lived being-in-the-world—one structured by a discursive or logical framework characteristic of thought and reason, and the other coupled with causal contingency and being affected, modes of connection to physical contingencies. Human paths through the world can be dissected in two distinct ways—one yields a narrative and the other *physis*, natural bringings-about, and they come together through autopoiesis, adaptation by progressive and dynamic self-formation (Gillett, 2008; Varela & Thompson, 2001). Rule-followers use their skills in dealing with truth-bearers or propositions to connect themselves with a domain of ideas or representations—*logos*— and to apply the results in their own cognitive structure and to the world of truth-makers or life as lived; we are *zoon logon echon*—the creature whose being is infused by the word (Heidegger). This thought underpins the "action structure" account of human action (Vallacher & Wegner, 1985) and lurks in debates about the reality of rule-following for an individual engaged in human practices of giving grounds, justifying what one is doing, and making projections based on the rules involved and past experience in applying them. Various accounts attempt to naturalise this skill through locating an individual in a collective but Wittgenstein's "Robinson"—the human individual living in isolation (Gillett, 1995), or any plausible developmental story in which a human child (perhaps relatively isolated) learns the skills involved in cognition provides a much better account of our entry into the space of reasons where we internalise and follow norms that allow us to tap into the tricks of representation meaning and thought (Gillett, 1992, 2008).

## 4     Meeting the Desiderata and Revisiting the Puzzles

The five desiderata for an account of the real enactive essence of human beings as conscious souls can now be assessed for its adequacy in responding to genuine philosophical concerns:

(a) *It should be a logically articulate conception and explain the A/P divide.*

Wittgenstein supports the need to say something more about human consciousness and the metaphysics of the soul when he speaks about "a piece of logical sleight of hand" (PI, #412):

> The feeling of an unbridgeable gulf between consciousness and brain process ... This idea of a difference in kind is accompanied by a slight giddiness—which occurs when we are performing a piece of logical sleight-of-hand.
> ... It is when I, for example, turn my attention in a particular way on my own consciousness, and, astonished, say to myself: THIS is supposed to be produced by a process in the brain!

In response we can focus on the truth conditions for a proposition of the type "X is conscious" and invoke the present enactive embodied view that consciousness is "on" when our neurocognitive capabilities and our embodied nature draw on our articulate, holistic, and flexible abilities to respond to the environment (drawing on interests, vulnerabilities, and saliencies informing a "hodological" map [Sartre] for reason-guided/discursively organised action).

What-it-is-like-to-be a human being therefore turns out to be complex:

1. The bruise factor refers to the actual way that things affect our bodies (the *tuche*);
2. the Othello in a nutshell problem refers to the potential cognitive richness and complexity that adds layers of meaning to every human experience; and
3. being a critter like me introduces vulnerabilities, abilities, and the shared imaginary into my cognitive engagement with diverse contexts.

They all concern *being there* (Clark, 1997) as intelligent protoplasm with flesh-and-blood sensibilities, coupled to the world, mediated by imagination, and expressed in a shared conceptual system produced as second nature develops. An answer to a what-is-it-like-to-be question cannot amount to actually having the experiences, nor could it capture the many ways in which we are intentionally engaged with things so as to induce a harmony on the myriad strings of the cerebral harp. We could say that poets, painters, novelists, and playwrights are constantly unfolding new aspects of what-it-is-like-to-be human, and even the closest species to us may be too unlike us given the difficulty we may have trying to understand "a stranger in a strange land" (Tomasello, 2014) or the possibility that "if a lion could speak, we could not understand him" (PI, 223e). Thus we need no fancy/fanciful metaphysics to account for the radical impenetrability of different varieties of what-it-is-like-to-be.

(b) *It should explain the evolutionary significance of consciousness.*

The enactive embodied view of consciousness is particularly apt for humans in the (much altered) world they have produced to live in. It combines explicit, or articulate, and inarticulate aspects of human consciousness. The latter are of two types: first, those that arise from being a critter like us, acquainted and causally interacting with the world in certain ways (the bruise factor and the *tuche* of Aristotle and Lacan); and second, the inarticulacy or indigestibility of our holistic lived experience ("nausea"—for Sartre or the *sticking of the signified in the gullet of the signifier* of Lacan).[3] This lived human trajectory is edited and summarised for its telling (to self and others) so that our desires—what move us—draw both on our embodiment and our symbolic allegiances (the former escape the selectivity and normatively constrained abstraction of propositionising). We are creatures of flesh impelled by desires and responsive to first nature and its urgings, but we are also moved by the imperatives imparted to us as we learn to speak and think and give an account of ourselves. Thus the affordances of things are shaped in part through speech as it illuminates our encounters with the world (Gillett, 1999). Words connect us to facts and a world shared by ourselves and others and conveyed between us through new combinations of words and the propositions they yield. This dual responsiveness to a world of representation and our being touched by it, working in concert, makes human consciousness unique in the animal kingdom.

(c) *It should show why consciousness is open to reason and reality.*

The enactive essence of consciousness is multiplex and autopoietic producing living, thinking beings engage in a physical world and equipped with complex cognitive systems that use imagery and imagination. Participation in the space of reasons turns innocence into experience through self-formation and inhibiting the call of the wild. JHJ, analysing consciousness, invoked a holistic set of diverse integrative neurocognitive skills drawing together four aspects of mental life: *will*—the ability to act thoughtfully and effectively, *memory*—the ability to use past experience to inform current activity, *reason*—the ability to codify or "propositionise" and reflect on experience, and *emotion*—reactions and sensibilities yoked into a world that affects us. These combine, on his account, as we represent and re-represent (and re-re-...) sensori-motor function involving the whole organism in its relation to the environment (1887). Our skills adapt us to the complex demands made of us and ground the internal relation between consciousness, the reality principle (the need to dynamically cognise a world shared with others), and moral capacity. Semantic structure and the connections between words—"the grammar of the word ... the post where the new word is stationed" (PI #257)—add complexity that massively extends online and offline processing by giving an individual access to a shared (storied) world of experience. That notional world binds us together and gives us a sense of the lives of others in ways that have huge affective influence on a human life in a world of contingency and causal impingements.

(d) *It should explain the "critters like us" intuition.*

Our coming to grips with a rich experiential world in which human mental life is elaborated and articulated is close to the heart of the reason why Wittgenstein remarks:

> What gives us *so much as the idea* that living beings, things, can feel? ...
> Only of what behaves like a human being can one say that it *has* pains.
> For one has to say it of a body, or, if you like, of a soul ...
> Think of the recognition of facial expressions Or of the description of facial expressions—which does not consist in giving the measurements of the face! Think, too. How one can imitate a man's face without seeing one's own in a mirror. (PI, 283–285)

Mirroring and intersubjectivity elaborate shared circuits of cognition. They form play into the neurocognitive basis of what Kant calls "mother wit" and are recruited into the panoply of cognitive re-re-representations that we use to confer meaning on life events and to guide our actions in the discursive space of reasons (Harre & Gillett, 1994; McDowell, 1996). Human cognition is therefore contoured to fit an objective, reflective, and normative domain requiring skills that straddle our participation in the space of reasons and the world of contingency.

Wittgenstein's cryptic remark, "if a lion could talk, we could not understand him" (PI, p223e), makes sense against this analytical framework—it hints that the intentional world of a lion (or other animals) may be so different from ours that its thought (if that can be ascribed absent a connection to the Fregean world of abstraction and the true and the good) is inaccessible to us. We "allocate cognitive resources" using cognitive skills arising in human forms of life, so that the many symbols and cultural icons that inform our view of the world would be a mystery to a lion as would its world, suffused by smells and urgencies, lacking names and naming, but rich in affects and intuitions, be to us. Our second nature has configured us so that, quite possibly, we could and would continuously and variously miss what the lion is noticing (and responding to) as we tentatively explored his domain and hoped not to meet him face to face.

(e) *It should clarify the link between being conscious and moral standing.*

A creature for whom things ought to be thus and so in ways dictated by discourse and normatively required in relation *to* that creature or *of* that creature has moral standing. That standing is tied up, however, with what he is conscious of. Consciousness informs the soul and gives us moral grounds for: (1) certain kinds of treatment (e.g. those that take account of enduring or future-directed interests) and (2) certain kinds of expectation (e.g. social responsibility and accountability in relation to the interests of others) and certain kinds of regard ("You may not care about her but you should in view of what has transpired."). When a creature responds in the highly complex way that demands we ascribe consciousness, one cannot lightly set aside that creature's experience as inconsequential and lacking any conception of its own ends. We therefore have to draw parallels between what certain experiences are like for that creature as it experiences and reasons about them and what similar experiences would be like for one of us and what significance would be attached to them. That single inclusive and imaginative step is the *fons et origo* of moral thought.

The current enactive embodied view of the soul notes that we conform ourselves to the requirements of a shared, discursive world and its ORN order. It is naturalistic, anthropological, and philosophically plausible and yields an adequate account of consciousness so as to provide a sound basis for understanding the relevance of second nature to the human soul as it analyses the way our intersubjective being creates a demanding experiential space for us to inhabit both doxastically and ethically.

Reifying metaphysics in terms of a flat-footed physicalism blinds us to the complex subtleties of human intersubjectivity and the meanings we create for ourselves and use in self-formation. Aristotle, however, notes that the various ways in which we integrate ourselves imply that we should not think of this multiplicity in terms of metaphysically distinct parts of the soul (as in dualism):

> The question might also be raised about the parts of the soul: What is the separate role of each in relation to the body? For, if the whole soul holds together the whole body, we should expect each part of the soul to hold together a part of the body. But this seems an impossibility; it is difficult even to imagine what sort of bodily part mind will hold together, or how it will do this.

But, all the same, in each of the bodily parts there are present all the parts of soul, and the souls so present are homogeneous with one another and with the whole; this means that the several parts of the soul are indisseverable from one another, although the whole soul is divisible. (DA 411b12–26)

The divisibility explored here must be conceptual if the argument is to be coherent, and it is clear that we are confronted with the insuperable problems of causal interaction if we approach the soul of a human being as anything other than a way of thinking about holistic embodied human experience. But our need to make distinctions so as to discuss the human intellect should not generate a metaphysics based on material objects and their functional parts:

We have no evidence as yet about mind or the power to think; it seems to be a widely different kind of soul, differing as what is eternal from what is perishable; it alone is capable of existence in isolation from all other psychic powers. All the other parts of soul, it is evident from what we have said, are, in spite of certain statements to the contrary, incapable of separate existence though, of course, distinguishable by definition. If opining is distinct from perceiving, to be capable of opining and to be capable of perceiving must be distinct, and so with all the other forms of living above enumerated. (DA 413b)

What is eternal are the laws of logic and mathematics—they transcend time and contingency and organise our reasoning in ways immune to temporal change. The problem comes to a sharp focus in the power to actively think as a conscious being attempting to make sense of a world of contingency where we are susceptible to the slings and arrows of outrageous fortune—there are multiple complex and interacting (neuro) cognitive functions discernible conceptually but inseparable in actual lived experience, aimed at mitigating the unpredictability and vulnerability that is the mark of flesh; the cognitive powers involved spring from "mother wit" but are refined by education to serve a harmony in the soul (*eudaimonea*):

The problem at once presents itself, in what sense we are to speak of parts of the soul, or how many we should distinguish. For in a sense there is an infinity of parts: it is not enough to distinguish, with some thinkers, the calculative, the passionate, and the desiderative, or with others the rational and the irrational; for if we take the dividing lines followed by these thinkers we shall find parts far more distinctly separated from one another than these, namely those we have just mentioned: (1) the nutritive, which belongs both to plants and to all animals, and (2) the sensitive, which cannot easily be classed as either irrational or rational; further (3) the imaginative, which is, in its being, different from all, while it is very hard to say with which of the others it is the same or not the same, supposing we determine to posit separate parts in the soul; and lastly (4) the appetitive, which would seem to be distinct both in definition and in power from all hitherto enumerated. (DA 432b)

The problem of divisions of the soul is clearly insuperable by simple-minded materialistic or object-based metaphysics, but is resolved through when we use a conceptual scalpel to dissect our being-in-the-world-with-others and set thinking apart from what is thought (and causally, physically engaged with). Aristotle uses the analogy of a line and our ability to think of it as having notional parts:

But that which mind thinks and the time in which it thinks are in this case divisible only incidentally and not as such. For in them too there is something indivisible (though, it may be, not isolable) which gives unity to the time and the whole of length; and this is found equally in every continuum whether temporal or spatial. (DA 430b)

The continuum which is the unity of consciousness is not based on a privileged and immaterial entity inhabiting its own corner of reality and contemplating itself, but as an intellectual necessity forced on us by the understanding and its need to make distinctions and comparisons within experience for the purpose of clarity of thought (Kant, B421). When that is clear, the artificial dissection of human function is seen to be compossible with neurally and conceptually integrated life as it is lived, so that offline (discursively inflected) processing is held in tension with the coupled being that sustains bodily life—actual living flesh and blood. We can then resist the temptation "to predicate of the thing that which lies in the method of representing it" (Wittgenstein, PI, #104). Our cognitive function does the tricky work of dissecting triply indirect responsivensss—to the self who acts, to the contingent world that acts on us, and to the world of abstraction and analysis—but it also holds in tension the fact that they are co-instantiated in a global cognitive workspace shaped by ontogeny—human upbringing.

And so our journey concludes with a return to the beginning and a sense of knowing that place more fully for the first time. Current philosophy and cognitive neuroscience often butts into a metaphysical thesis that leads discussions of consciousness and the human soul into an impasse. An active embodied theory of mind, supplemented by contemporary neuroscience and the concept of dynamic non-linear neural processing measured by (e.g.) wMSI, picks up strands of thought implicit in Aristotle and Brentano and glimpsed in thinkers as diverse as Kant, Wittgenstein, and Foucault. These analyses link second nature, the human soul, and our being in communities ("kingdoms of ends") and indicate a way forward through phenomenologically informed cognitive neuroscience and philosophy of mind to a neurophilosophy that has implications for meta-ethics and the normativity of social and political thought, but those exciting possibilities take us into territory beyond the scope of the present work.

## 5   RECAP ON CHAPTER 7

Full-blooded Aristotelianism. A properly filled-out and neurologically informed Aristotelian naturalism takes us beyond ethological interactions at a straightforward natural level and into the interactive and nuanced world of discourse to yield a form of discursive naturalism in which argument and socio-political engagement help shape the human mind. At that level our relationships, attributions, and valuing of each other become an important part of the picture, but not spooky or mysterious beyond the point of analysis and argument. The full-blooded view that results is completely compatible with a form of discursively informed anti-reductive naturalism that lays our attunement to a shared world open to intellectual inquiry.

### NOTES

1. The phrase is used by Janet frame and regarded as evidence that she is insane by her concerned, and prosaic, family members.
2. The cruelty here is directly related to Antonin Artaud's "theatre of cruelty."
3. The expression is from Lacan (FFCP, 270).

### REFERENCES AND BIBLIOGRAPHY

Barthes, R. (1972). *Mythologies*. New York: Hill and Wang.
Block, N. (1995). On a confusion about a function of consciousness. *Behavioral and Brain Sciences, 18*, 227–247.

Cassam, Q. (1997). *Self and world*. Oxford: Oxford University Press.

Church, J. (1995). Fallacies or analyses? *Behavioral and Brain Sciences, 18*, 251–252.

Clark, A. (1997). *Being there: Putting brain body and world together again*. Cambridge, MA: MIT Press.

Gillett, G. (1992). *Representation, meaning and thought*. Oxford: Clarendon.

Gillett, G. (1995). Humpty Dumpty and the night of the triffids: Individualism and rule-following. *Synthese, 105*, 191–206.

Gillett, G. (1999). The evolutionary foothills of the mind. *Philosophy, 74*, 331–360.

Gillett, G. (2008). *Subjectivity and being somebody: Human identity and neuroethics* (St Andrews Series on Philosophy and Public Affairs). Exeter: Imprint Academic.

Harre, R., & Gillett, G. (1994). *The discursive mind*. London: Sage.

Jackson, F. (1986). What Mary didn't know. *Journal of Philosophy, 83*(5), 291–295.

McDowell, J. (1996). *Mind and world* (2nd ed.). Cambridge, MA: Harvard University Press.

Morton, A. (1995). Phenomenal and attentional consciousness may be inextricable. *Behavioral and Brain Sciences, 18*, 263–264.

Snowdon, P. (2014). *Persons, animals, ourselves*. Oxford: Oxford University Press.

Thompson, E., & Varela, F. (2001). Radical embodiment: Neural dynamics and consciousness. *Trends in Cognitive Science, 5*(10), 416–425.

Tomasello, M. (2014). *The natural history of human thinking*. Cambridge, MA: Harvard University Press.

Tye, M. (1999). Phenomenal consciousness: The explanatory gap as a cognitive illusion. *Mind, 108*, 705–726.

Vallacher, R. R., & Wegner, D. M. (1985). *A theory of action identification*. Hove: Lawrence Ehrlbaum & Associates.

Zahavi, D. (2013) Intentionality and phenomenology: Phenomenological take on the hard problem. *Canadian Journal of Philosophy* 32 (Suppl) 63-92.

# REFERENCES AND BIBLIOGRAPHY

Adams, F., Drebushenko, D., Fuller, G., & Stecker, R. (1990). Narrow content: Fodor's folly. *Mind & Language, 5*(3), 214–229.

Allport, A. (1993). Visual attention. In M. I. Posner (Ed.), *Foundations of cognitive science* (pp. 631–682). Cambridge, MA: MIT Press.

Andorfer, J. C. (1985). Multiple personality in the human information-processor: A case history and theoretical formulation. *Journal of Clinical Psychology, 41*(3), 309–324.

Apperly, I., Samson, D. E., & Humphreys, G. W. (2005). Domain specificity and theory of mind: Evaluating neuropsychological evidence. *Trends in Cognitive Neuroscience, 9*(12), 572–577.

Aristotle. (1925). *Nichomachean ethics* (D. Ross, Trans.). Oxford: Oxford University Press. [NE].

Aristotle. (1986). [DA]: *De Anima* (On the soul) Aristotle (ca. 350 BC) (J. A. Smith, Trans.). *Bekker page numbers are given in square brackets* [http://psych-classics.yorku.ca/Aristotle/De-anima/index.htm] also (H. Lawson Tancred, Trans.). Harmondsworth: Penguin.

Armstrong, D. (2004). *Truth and truthmakers*. Cambridge: Cambridge University Press.

Arras, J. (2001). Free standing pragmatism in law and bioethics. *Theoretical Medicine and Bioethics, 22*(2), 69–85.

Augstein, M. (1996). J C Prichard's concept of moral insanity—A medical theory of the corruption of human nature. *Medical History, 40*(3), 311–343.

Baars, B. (2002). The conscious access hypothesis: Origins and recent evidence. *Trends in Cognitive Science, 6*(1), 47–52.

© The Author(s) 2018

G. Gillett, *From Aristotle to Cognitive Neuroscience*,
https://doi.org/10.1007/978-3-319-93635-2

Baron-Cohen, S. (1995). *Mindblindness.* Cambridge, MA: MIT Press.

Barsalou, L., Brezeal, C., & Smith, L. (2007). Cognition as coordinated non-cognition. *Cognitive Process, 8,* 79–91.

Barthes, R. (1972). *Mythologies.* New York: Hill and Wang.

Bartolomeo, P. (2002). The relationship between visual perception and visual mental imagery: A reappraisal of the neuropsychological evidence. *Cortex, 38*(3), 357–378.

Bauer, R. M. (1984). Autonomic recognition of names and faces in prosopagnosia: A neuropsychological application of the guilty knowledge test. *Neuropsychologia, 22,* 457–469.

Bayne, T. (2008). The phenomenology of agency. *Philosophy Compass, 3*(1), 182–202.

Blackburn, S. (1984). *Spreading the word.* Oxford: Clarendon.

Blair, J. (2003). Neurobiological basis of psychopathy. *British Journal of Psychiatry, 182,* 5–7.

Blair, R. J. R. (2004). The roles of orbito-frontal cortex in the modulation of anti-social behaviour. *Brain and Cognition, 55,* 198–208.

Blair, R. J. R. (2007). The amygdala and ventromedial frontal cortex in morality and psychopathy. *Trends in Cognitive Sciences, 13*(9), 387–392.

Block, N. (1995). On a confusion about a function of consciousness. *Behavioral and Brain Sciences, 18,* 227–247.

Block, N. (2001). Paradox and cross purposes in recent work on consciousness. *Cognition, 79,* 197–219.

Bolton, D., & Hill, J. (1996). *Mind, meaning and mental disorder.* Oxford: Oxford University Press.

Brentano, F. (1874 [1973]). *Psychology from an empirical standpoint* (L. McAlister, Trans.). London: Routledge & Kegan Paul.

Brentano, F. (1929 [1981]). *Sensory and noetic consciousness* (M. Schattle & L. McAlister, Trans.). London: Routledge and Kegan Paul.

Bruner, J. (1990). *Acts of meaning.* Cambridge, MA: Harvard University Press.

Cassam, Q. (1997). *Self and world.* Oxford: Oxford University Press.

Caston, V. (1996). Why Aristotle needs imagination. *Phronesis, 41,* 20–55.

Chamberlain, S., et al. (2008). Orbitofrontal dysfunction in patients with obsessive compulsive disorder. *Science, 321,* 421–422.

Chemero, A. (2003). An outline of a theory of affordances. *Ecological Psychology, 15*(2), 181–185.

Chemero, A. (2009). *Radical embodied cognitive science.* Cambridge, MA: MIT Press.

Chemero, A. (2011). *Radical embodied cognitive science.* Cambridge, MA: MIT Press.

Chomsky, N. (2006). *Language and mind* (3rd ed.). Cambridge: Cambridge University Press.

Church, J. (1995). Fallacies or analyses? *Behavioral and Brain Sciences, 18,* 251–252.

Clark, A. (1997). *Being there: Putting brain body and world together again.* Cambridge, MA: MIT Press.

Clark, A. (2008). *Supersizing the mind: Embodiment, action and cognitive extension.* Oxford: Oxford University Press.

Confer, W. N., & Ables, B. S. (1983). *Multiple personality: Aetiology, diagnosis and treatment.* New York: Human Sciences Press.

Cornell, D. G., Warren, J., Hawk, G., & Stafford, E. (1996). Psychopathy in instrumental and reactive violent offenders. *Journal of Consulting and Clinical Psychology, 64*(4), 783–790.

Cranford, R. (1988). The Persistent Vegetative State: The medical reality (getting the facts straight). *The Hastings Center Report, 18*(1), 27–28.

Cranford, R., & Smith, R. D. (1988). Consciousness: The most critical moral (constitutional) standard for human personhood. *American Journal of Law and Medicine, 13,* 233–248.

Csikszentmihalyi, M. (1990). *Flow: The psychology of optimal experience.* New York: Harper & Row.

Cussins, A. Content, embodiment and objectivity: The theory of cognitive trails. *Mind, 101,* 651–688.

Damasio, A. (1996). The somatic marker hypothesis and the possible functions of the prefrontal cortex. *Philosophical Transactions of the Royal Society of London, 351,* 1413–1429.

Damasio, A. (2010). *Self comes to mind.* New York: Random House.

Danto, A. (1964). The artworld. *The Journal of Philosophy, 61*(19), 571–584.

Dapretto, M., Davies, M., et al. (2006). Understanding emotions in others: Mirror neuron dysfunction in children with autism spectrum disorders. *Nature Neuroscience, 9*(1), 28–30.

Davidson, D. (1980). *Essays on actions and events.* Oxford: Clarendon.

Davidson, D. (2001). *Subjective, intersubjective, objective.* Oxford: Oxford University Press.

Davis, J., Gillett, G., & Kozma, R. (2015). Revisiting Brentano on consciousness: A striking correlation with ECoG findings about the action-perception cycle and the emergence of knowledge and meaning. *Mind and Matter, 13*(1), 45–69.

Davis, J., Gillett, G., & Kozma, R. (2016). Brentano on consciousness: A striking correlation with ECOG findings about the cognitive cycle and the emergence of knowledge and meaning. *Mind and Matter, 13*(1), 12–27.

Dehaene, S. (2014). *Consciousness and the brain.* London: Penguin..

Dehaene, S., & Changeux, J. P. (2011). Experimental and theoretical approaches to conscious processing. *Neuron, 70,* 200–227.

Dehaene, S., & Naccache, L. (2001). Towards a cognitive neuroscience of consciousness: Basic evidence and a workspace framework. *Cognition, 79,* 1–37.

Dennett, D. (1978). *Brainstorms*. Cambridge, MA: MIT Press.

Dennett, D. (1991). *Consciousness explained*. London: Penguin.

Dennett, D. (2003). *Freedom evolves*. London: Penguin.

Derdikman, D., & Moser, E. (2010). A manifold of spatial maps in the brain. *Trends in Cognitive Science, 14*(12), 561–569.

Dewey, J. (1934). *Art as experience*. New York: Minton, Balch & Co.

Di Dio, C., & Gallese, V. (2009). Neuroaesthetics: A review. *Current Opinion in Neurobiology, 19,* 682–687.

Di Dio, C., Macaluso, E., & Rizzoletti, G. (2007). The golden beauty: Brain response to classical and renaissance sculpture. *PLoS One, 11,* e1201.

Dreyfus, H. L. (2014). *Skillful coping* (M. Wrathall, Ed.). Oxford: Oxford University Press.

Dreyfus, H., & Taylor, C. (2015). *Retrieving realism*. Cambridge, MA: Harvard University Press.

Dunbar, R., & Schulz, S. (2007). Evolution in the social brain. *Science, 317,* 1344–1347.

Edelman, G. (1992). *Bright air, brilliant fire: On the matter if the mind*. London: Penguin.

Elliot, C. (2003). *Slow cures and bad philosophers*. Durham, NC: Duke University Press.

Ellis, H. D., & Lewis, M. B. (2001). Capgras delusion: A window on face recognition. *Trends in Cognitive Neuroscience, 5*(4), 149–156.

Ellis, R., & Newton, N. (2010). *How the mind uses the brain: To move the body and image the universe*. Chicago: Open Court Publishers.

Evans, G. (1982). *The varieties of reference*. Oxford: Clarendon.

Foot, P. (2001). *Natural goodness*. Oxford: Oxford University Press.

Foucault, M. (1984). *The Foucault reader* (P. Rabinow, Ed.). London: Penguin.

Foucault, M. (2008). *Introduction to Kant's anthropology*. Los Angeles: Semiotexte (FKA).

Franz, E. A. (2010). A framework for conceptual binding of bimanual actions: Possible applications to neurology and neuro-rehabilitative therapies. *Current Trends in Neurology, 4,* 1–22.

Franz, E. A., & Gillett, G. (2011). John Hughlings Jackson's evolutionary neurology: A unifying framework for cognitive neuroscience. *Brain, 134,* 3114–3120.

Freeman, W. (1994). Neural networks and chaos. *Journal of Theoretical Biology, 171,* 13–18.

Freeman, W. (2000). A neurobiological interpretation of semiotics: Meaning, representation and intention. *Information Sciences, 124,* 93–102.

Freeman, W. J. (2008). Nonlinear brain dynamics and intention according to Aquinas. *Mind and Matter, 6*(2), 207–234.

Freeman, W. J. (2015). Mechanism and significance of global coherence in scalp EEG. *Current Opinion in Biology, 23,* 199–205.

Frege, G. (1977). *Logical investigations* (P. Geach, Trans. & Ed.) Oxford: Blackwell.

Frege, G. (1980). *Translations from the philosophical writings of Gottlob Frege* (P. Geach & M. Black, Eds.). Oxford: Blackwell.

Freud, S. (1986). *The essentials of psychoanalysis* (J. Strachey, Trans.). Harmondsworth: Penguin.

Friedlander, L., & Desrocher, M. (2006). Neuroimaging studies of obsessive-compulsive disorder in adults and children. *Clinical Psychology Review, 26,* 32–49.

Friston, K. (2010). The free energy principle: A unified brain theory? *Nature Reviews/Neuroscience, 11,* 127–134.

Fukuda, M., Hata, A., et al. (1996). Event-related potential correlates of functional hearing loss; Reduced P3 amplitude with preserved N1 and N2 components in a unilateral case. *Psychiatry and Clinical Neurosciences, 50*(2), 85–87.

Fullinwinder, S. (1983). Sigmund Freud, Hughlings Jackson and speech. *Journal of the History of Ideas, 44*(1), 151–158.

Gallagher, S. (2005). *How the body shapes the mind*. Oxford: Oxford University Press.

Gardner, H. (1974). *The shattered mind*. New York: Vintage.

Gazzaniga, M. (1970). *The bisected brain*. New York: Appleton Century Crofts.

Gazzaniga, M. (2005). Forty five years of split brain research and still going strong. *Nature Neuroscience, 4,* 853–869.

Gendler, T. S. (2008). Alief and belief. *The Journal of Philosophy, 105,* 634–663.

Gibson, J. J. (1979). *The ecological approach to visual perception*. Boston: Houghton Mifflin.

Gillett, G. (1987). Concepts, structures and meaning. *Inquiry, 30,* 101–112.

Gillett, G. (1991). The neurophilosophy of pain. *Philosophy, 66,* 191–206.

Gillett, G. (1992). *Representation, meaning and thought*. Oxford: Clarendon.

Gillett, G. (1993). Ought and wellbeing. *Inquiry, 36,* 287–306.

Gillett, G. (1995). Humpty Dumpty and the night of the triffids: Individualism and rule-following. *Synthese, 105,* 191–206.

Gillett, G. (1997). Husserl, Wittgenstein and the snark. *Philosophy and Phenomenological Research, LVII,* 331–350.

Gillett, G. (1999). The evolutionary foothills of the mind. *Philosophy, 74,* 331–360.

Gillett, G. (2001). Intention and agency. In N. Naffine, R. Owens, & J. Williams (Eds.), *Intention in law and philosophy* (pp. 57–69). Burlington: Ashgate.

Gillett, G. (2001). Signification and the unconscious and "Response to Read". *Philosophical Psychology, 14*(4), 477–498; 515–518.

Gillett, G. (2004). *Bioethics and the clinic: Hippocratic reflections*. Baltimore, MD: Johns Hopkins University Press.

Gillett, G. (2008). *Subjectivity and being somebody: Human identity and neuroethics* (St Andrews Series on Philosophy and Public Affairs). Exeter: Imprint Academic.

Gillett, G. (2009). *The mind and its discontents* (2nd ed.). Oxford: Oxford University Press.

Gillett, G. (2010). Intentional action, moral responsibility and psychopaths. In L. Malatesti & J. McMillan (Eds.), *Responsibility and psychopathy: Interfacing law, ethics, and psychiatry* (pp. 283–298). Oxford: Oxford University Press.

Gillett, G. (2014a). Review of Robert Kirk "The conceptual link from mental to physical". *Philosophy, 89,* 352–357. https://doi.org/10.1017/S0031819113000636

Gillett, G. (2014b). Concepts, consciousness and counting by pigeons. *Mind, 123,* 1147–1153.

Gillett, G. (2015). Culture, truth, and science after Lacan. *Journal of Bioethical Inquiry, 12,* 633–644.

Gillett, G., & Amos C. (2015). The discourse of clinical ethics and the maladies of the soul. In *Oxford handbook of psychiatric ethics* (Vol. I, Chap. 30). Oxford: Oxford University Press.

Gillett, G., & Copeland, P. (2003). The bioethical structure of a human being. *Journal of Applied Philosophy, 12*(2), 123–132.

Gillett, G., & Franz, L. (2014). Evolutionary neurology, responsive equilibrium, and the moral brain. *Consciousness and Cognition.* Retrieved from http://www.sciencedirect.com/science/article/pii/S105381001400172X

Gillett, G., & Harre, R. (2013). Discourse and diseases of the psyche. In K. W. M. Fulford et al. (Eds.), *The Oxford handbook of philosophy and psychiatry* (pp. 307–320). Oxford: Oxford University Press.

Gillett, G., & Liu, S. (2012). Free will and Necker's cube: Reason, language and top-down control in cognitive neuroscience. *Philosophy, 87*(1), 29–50.

Gillett, G., & McMillan, J. (2001). *Consciousness and intentionality.* Amsterdam: John Benjamins.

Glannon, W. (2015). *Free will and the brain.* Cambridge: Cambridge University Press.

Gleitman, H. (1991). *Psychology* (3rd ed.). New York: Norton.

Greene, J. (2003). From neural 'is' to moral 'ought': What are the moral implications of neuroscientific moral psychology? *Nature Neuroscience, 4,* 847–850.

Greene, J., & Haidt, J. (2002). How (and where) does moral judgment work? *Trends in Cognitive Neuroscience, 6*(12), 517–523.

Gregory, R. (1966). *Eye and brain.* London: Weidenfeld and Nicholson.

Griffiths, P. (1997). *What emotions really are.* Chicago: University of Chicago Press.

Hacking, I. (1995). *Rewriting the soul.* Princeton, NJ: Princeton University Press.

Hacking, I. (2004). *Historical ontology.* Cambridge, MA: Harvard University Press.

Haggard, P. (2008). Human volition: Towards a neuroscience of will. *Nature Reviews Neuroscience, 9*, 934–946.

Haidt, J. (2001). The emotional dog and its rational tail: A social intuitionist approach to moral judgment. *Psychological Review, 108*(4), 814–834.

Haldane, J. (1992). Aquinas and the active intellect. *Philosophy, 67*, 199–210.

Hamlyn, D. (1973). Human learning. In R. Peters (Ed.), *The philosophy of education* (pp. 178–194). Oxford: Oxford University Press.

Hare, R., & Neumann, C. (2010). Psychopathy, assessment and forensic implications. In L. Malatesti & J. McMillan (Eds.), *Responsibility and psychopathy* (pp. 93–124). Oxford: Oxford University Press.

Harre, R., & Gillett, G. (1994). *The discursive mind.* London: Sage.

Harris, J. C. (2003). Social neuroscience, empathy, brain integration and neurodevelopmental disorders. *Physiology and Behavior, 79*, 525–531.

Heidegger, M. (1953 [1996]). *Being and time* (J. Stambaugh, Trans.). New York: SUNY Press.

Hemphill, J. F., Hare, R. D., & Wong, S. (1998). Psychopathy and recidivism a review. *Legal and Criminological Psychology, 3*, 737–745 Blair (2003).

Howard, J. E., & Dorfman, L. J. (1986). Evoked potentials in hysteria and malingering. *Journal of Clinical Neurophysiology, 3*(1), 39–49.

Hubbs, G. (2013). Alief and explanation. *Metaphilosophy, 44*(5), 604–620.

Hughlings Jackson, J. (1878). On affectations of speech from disease of the brain (1). *Brain, I*(III), 304–330.

Hughlings Jackson, J. (1879). On affectations of speech from disease of the brain (2). *Brain, I*(III), 203–222.

Hughlings Jackson, J. (1884). Croonian lectures on the evolution and dissolution of the nervous system. *Lancet*: (a) March 29, pp. 555–558; (b) April 12, pp. 649–652; and (c) 26, pp. 739–744.

Hughlings Jackson, J. (1887). Remarks on the evolution and dissolution of the nervous system. *British Journal of Psychiatry, 33*, 25–48.

Hume, D. (1740 [1969]). *A treatise of human nature* (E. Mossner, Ed.). London: Penguin.

Hurford, J. R. (2003). The neural basis of predicate-argument structure. *Behavioral and Brain Sciences, 26*, 261–316.

Hurley, S. (1998). *Consciousness in action.* Cambridge, MA: Harvard University Press.

Hurley, S. (2008). The shared circuits model (SCM): How control, mirroring, and simulation can enable imitation, deliberation and mindreading. *Behavioral and Brain Sciences, 31*, 1–58.

Husserl, E. (1950 [1999]). *Cartesian meditations* (D. Cairns, Trans.). Dordrecht: Kluwer.

Husserl, E. (1954 [1970]). *The crisis of European sciences and transcendental phenomenology* (D. Carr, Trans.). Chicago: Northwestern University Press.

Husserl, E. (1958 [1913]). *Ideas* (W. R. Boyce Gibson, Trans.). London: Allen and Unwin (hereinafter *Ideas* [G]. OR (1982 [1913]) *Ideas pertaining to a pure phenomenology and to a phenomenological philosophy* (F. Kersten, Trans.). The Hague: Martinus Nijhoff.

Husserl, E. (1982). *Ideas pertaining to a pure phenomenology and to a phenomenological philosophy* (F. Kersten, Trans.). The Hague: Martinus Nijhoff.

Ishai, A. (2008). Let's face it: It's a cortical network. *Neuroimage, 40,* 415–419.

Jackson, F. (1986). What Mary didn't know. *Journal of Philosophy, 83*(5), 291–295.

Jacquette, D. (2004). *The Cambridge companion to Brentano.* Cambridge, UK: Cambridge University Press.

James, W. (1892 [2011]). The stream of consciousness (First published in *Psychology*, Chapter XI) 1892. Retrieved March 23, 2015, from http://cosmology.com/Consciousness121.html

James, W. (1909 [2012]). *A pluralistic universe.* The Floating Press. Retrieved from http://thefloatingpress.com/

Jaynes, J. (1989). Verbal hallucinations and precomscious mentality. In M. Spitzer & B. Maher (Eds.), *Philosophy and psycholpathology.* New York: Springer-Verlag.

Jaynes, J. (1990). *The origin of consciousness in the breakdown of the bicameral mind.* New York: Houghton Mifflin.

Jennett, B., & Plum, F. (1972). Persistent vegetative state after brain damage. *The Lancet, 1,* 734–737.

Kamber, R. (1998). Weitz reconsidered: A clearer view of why theories of art fail. *British Journal of Aesthetics, 38*(8), 33–46.

Kant, I. (1788 [1956]). *The critique of practical reason* (L. W. Beck, Trans.). Indianapolis: Bobbs Merrill (hereinafter C PracR).

Kant, I. (1789 [1929]). *The critique of pure reason* (N. Kemp Smith, Trans.). London: Macmillan, or Tr. P. Guyer & A. Wood, Cambridge, UK: Cambridge University Press (hereinafter CPR; references will be given by B pagination eg B562 unless the passage only exists in the A edition).

Kant, I. (1793 [1953]). *Critique of judgment* (J. H. Bernard, Trans.). New York: Hafner (hereinafter CJ).

Kant, I. (1798 [1978]). *Anthropology from a pragmatic point of view* (V. L. Dodwell, Trans.). Carbondale: Southern Illinois University Press (hereinafter A).

Kanwisher, N., McDermott, J., & Chun, M. M. (1997). The fusiform face area: A module in Human extrastriate cortex specialized for face perception. *Journal of Neuroscience, 17*(11), 4302–4311.

Karmiloff-Smith, A. (1992). *Beyond modularity.* Cambridge, MA: MIT Press.

Kiehl, K., et al. (2001). Limbic abnormalities in affective processing by criminal psychopaths as revealed by functional magnetic resonance imaging. *Biological Psychiatry, 50,* 677–684.

Kim, J. (2010). *Essays in the metaphysics of mind.* Oxford: Oxford University Press.

King, J. R., Sitt, J. D., Faugeras, F., Rohaut, B., El Karoui, I., Cohen, L., et al. (2013). Information sharing in the brain indexes consciousness in noncommunicative patients. *Current Biology, 23,* 1914–1919.

Klimesch, W. (1999). EEG alpha and theta oscillations reflect cognitive and memory performance a review and analysis. *Brain Research Reviews, 29,* 169–195.

Knott, A. (2012). *Sensorimotor cognition and natural language syntax.* Cambridge, MA: MIT Press.

Kolb, B., & Wishaw, I. (1990). *The fundamentals of human neuropsychology.* New York: W.H.Freeman & Co.

Kozma, R., Davies, J., & Freeman, W. J. (2012). Synchronized minima in ECoG power at frequencies between beta-gamma oscillations disclose cortical singularities in cognition. *Journal of Neuroscience and Neuroengineering, 1*(1), 11.

Kripke, S. (1982). *Wittgenstein on rules and private language.* Oxford: Blackwell.

Kwon, J. S., et al. (2003). Neural correlates of clinical symptoms and cognitive dysfunctions in obsessive-compulsive disorder. *Psychiatry Research: Neuroimaging, 122,* 37–47.

Lacan, J. (1977). *Ecrits* (A. Sheridan, Trans.). New York: Norton & Co.

Lacan, J. (1981). *The four fundamental concepts of psychoanalysis.* London: Norton & Co.

Lamm, C., Batson, C. D., & Decety, J. (2007). The neural substrate of human empathy: Effects of perspective taking and cognitive appraisal. *Journal of Cognitive Neuroscience, 19*(1), 42–58.

Levinas, E. (1996). *Basic philosophical writings* (A. Peperzak, S. Critchley, & R. Bernasconi, Eds.). Bloomington: Indiana University Press.

Levine, J. (1995). Phenomenal access: A moving target. *Behavioral and Brain Sciences, 18,* 261.

Levy, N. (2014). *Consciousness and moral responsibility.* Oxford: Oxford University Press.

Libet, B. (1985). Unconscious cerebral initiative and the role of conscious will in voluntary action. *The Behavioural and Brain Sciences, 8,* 529–566.

Locke, J. (1689 [1975]). *An essay concerning human understanding* (P. Nidditch, Ed.). Oxford: Clarendon, 1975 (hereinafter EHU).

Locke, J. (1789). *An essay concerning human understanding.* Oxford: Oxford University Press.

Lovibond, S. (1983). *Realism and imagination in ethics.* Oxford: Blackwell.

Lovibond, S. (2002). *Ethical formation.* Cambridge, MA: Harvard University Press.

Luria, A. R. (1973). *The working brain.* Harmondsworth: Penguin.

Lynam, D., & Gudonis, L. (2005). The development of psychopathy. *Annual Review of Clinical Psychology, 1,* 381–407.

Maibom, H. (2005). Moral unreason: The case of psychopathy. *Mind and Language, 29,* 237–257.

McDowell, J. (1994). *Mind and world*. Cambridge, MA: Harvard University Press.

McDowell, J. (1996). *Mind and world* (2nd ed.). Cambridge, MA: Harvard University Press.

McDowell, J. (1998). *Mind, value and reality*. Cambridge, MA: Harvard University Press.

McGilchrist, I. (2010). *The master and his emissary*. New Haven, CT: Yale University Press.

McGuigan, F. J. (1997). A neuromuscular model of mind with clinical and educational applications. *Journal of Mind and Behavior, 18*(4), 351–370.

Meares, R., Hampshire, R., Gordon, E., & Kraiuhin, C. (1985). Whose hysteria; Briquet's, Janet's or Freud's? *Australian and New Zealand Journal of Psychiatry, 19*, 256–263.

Mercier, H., & Sperber, D. (2011). Why do humans reason? Arguments for an argumentative theory. *Behavioural and Brain Sciences, 34*, 57–111.

Merleau-Ponty, M. (1962). *The phenomenology of perception* (C. Smith, Trans.). London: Routledge.

Merleau-Ponty, M. (1973). *Consciousness and the acquisition of language* (H. Silverman, Trans.). Chicago: Northwestern University Press.

Mitchell, J. P. (2009). Social psychology as a natural kind. *Trends in Cognitive Science, 13*(5), 246–251.

Morton, A. (1995). Phenomenal and attentional consciousness may be inextricable. *Behavioral and Brain Sciences, 18*, 263–264.

Motzkin, J. C., Newman, J. P., Kiehl, K. A., & Koenigs, M. (2011). Reduced prefrontal connectivity in psychopathy. *Journal of Neuroscience, 31*(4), 17348–17357.

Mullen, R., & Gillett, G. (2014). Delusions: A different kind of belief. *Philosophy, Psychiatry & Psychology 23*, 27–38; Delusions and the postures of the mind. *Philosophy, Psychiatry & Psychology 23*, 47–50.

Murdoch, I. (1986). *Acastos*. London: Chatto & Windus.

Nagel, T. (1979). *Mortal questions*. Cambridge: Cambridge University Press.

Navon, D. (1995). Consciousness, the local newspaper of the mind. *Behavioral and brain sciences, 18*, 265.

Neisser, U. (1976). *Cognition and reality*. San Francisco: Freeman.

Neisser, U. (1982). *Memory observed*. San Francisco: W.H. Freeman & Co.

Noe, A. (2009). *Out of our heads*. New York: Hill & Wang.

Noe, A., & Thompson, E. (2004). Are there neural correlates of consciousness? *Journal of Consciousness Studies, 11*, 3–28.

Northoff, G., & Bermpohl, F. (2004). Cortical midline structures and the self. *Trends in Cognitive Neuroscience, 8*, 102–107.

Nussbaum, M. (1990). *Love's knowledge*. Oxford: Oxford University Press.

O'Regan, J. K., & Noe, A. (2001). A sensorimotor account of vision and visual consciousness. *Brain and Behavioural Sciences, 24*, 939–973.

Palvaa, J. M., Montoa, S., Kulashekhara, S., & Palva, S. (2010). Neuronal synchrony reveals working memory and predicts individual memory capacity. *Proceedings of the National Academy of Sciences, 107,* 7580–7585.

Parfit, D. (1984). *Reasons and persons.* Oxford: Clarendon.

Parkin, A. (1996). *Explorations in cognitive neuropsychology.* Oxford: Blackwell.

Paulhus, D., & Williams, K. (2002). The dark triad of personality: Narcissism, Machiavellianism, and psychopathy. *Journal of Research in Personality, 36,* 556–563.

Pinker, S. (2010). The cognitive niche: Coevolution of intelligence, sociality and language. *Proceedings of the National Academy of Sciences, 107*(s2), 8993–8999.

Pinker, S. (2011). *The better angels of our nature.* New York: Allen Lane.

Raine, A. (2002). Biosocial studies of antisocial and violent behavior in children and adults: A review. *Journal of Abnormal Child Psychology, 30*(4), 311–326.

Ramachandran, V. S., & Blakeslee, S. (1998). *Phantoms in the brain.* New York: William Morrow.

Ratcliffe, M. (2009). Understanding existential changes in psychiatric illness: The indispensability of phenomenology. In M. Broome & L. Bertilotti (Eds.), *Psychiatry as cognitive neuroscience* (pp. 224–244). Oxford: Oxford University Press.

Rawls, J. (1957). Outline of a decision procedure for ethics. *Philosophical Review, 66,* 177–197.

Rist, J. (1966). Notes on Aristotle De Anima 3.5. *Classical Philology, 61,* 8–20.

Robinson, D. (1989). *Aristotle's psychology.* New York: Columbia University Press.

Rosen, R. (1985). *Anticipatory systems: Philosophical, mathematical, and methodological foundations.* New York: Pergamum.

Roskies, A. (2006). Neuroscientific challenges to free will and responsibility. *Trends in Cognitive Science, 10*(9), 419–423.

Russell, B. (1988). *On the nature of acquaintance* (pp. 125–174) (reprinted in *Logic and knowledge*). London: Unwin.

Sacks, O. (1985). *The man who mistook his wife for a hat.* London: Duckworth.

Sartre, J. P. (1958). *Being and nothingness* (H. Barnes, Trans.). London: Methuen & Co.

Sartre, J. P. (1971). *Sketch for a theory of the emotions* (P. Mairet, Trans.). London: Methuen & Co.

Sass, L., & Parnas, J. (2007). Explaining schizophrenia: The relevance of phenomenology. In M. C. Chung, K. W. M. Fulford, & G. Graham (Eds.), *Reconceiving schizophrenia* (pp. 63–96). Oxford: Oxford University Press.

Saxe, R. (2006). Uniquely human social cognition. *Current Opinion in Neurobiology, 16,* 235–239.

Saxe, R., & Wexler, A. (2005). Making sense of another mind: The role of the right temporo-parietal junction. *Neuropsychologia, 43,* 1391–1399.

Searle, J. (1992). *The rediscovery of the mind.* Cambridge, MA: MIT Press.

Sekuler, R., & Blake, R. (1994). *Perception* (3rd ed.). New York: McGraw-Hill.

Sellars, W. (1997). *Empiricism and the philosophy of mind*. Cambridge, MA: Harvard University Press.

Shapiro, D. (1965). *Neurotic styles*. New York: Basic Books.

Singer, T. (2004). Empathy for pain involves the affective but not sensory aspects of pain. *Science, 305*, 1157–1162.

Singer, T. (2006). The neuronal basis and ontogeny of empathy and mind reading: Review of literature and implications for future research. *Neuroscience & Biobehavioural Reviews, 30*, 855–862.

Snowdon, P. (2014). *Persons, animals, ourselves*. Oxford: Oxford University Press.

Sorabji, R. (1974). Body and soul in Aristotle. *Philosophy, 49*, 63–89.

Spence, S. A., Hunter, M. D., & Harpin, G. (2002). Neuroscience and the will. *Current Opinion in Psychiatry, 15*(5), 519–526.

Sperry, R. W. (1977). Forebrain commuissurotomy and conscious awareness. *Journal of Medicine and Philosophy, 2*(2), 100–126.

Sperry, R. (1984). Consciousness, personal identity and the divided brain. *Neuropsychologia, 22*, 661–673.

Spitzer, M. (1999). *The mind within the net*. Cambridge, MA: MIT Press.

Stanghellini, G. (2004). *Disembodied spirits and deanimated bodies*. Oxford: Oxford University Press.

Stephens, G., & Graham, G. (1994). Self consciousness, mental agency, and the clinical psychopathology of thought insertion. *Philosophy, Psychiatry and Psychology, 1*, 1–12.

Stephens, G. L., & Graham, G. (2000). *When self-consciousness breaks*. Cambridge, MA: MIT Press.

Sterelney, K. (2013). *The evolved apprentice: How evolution made human beings unique*. Cambridge, MA: MIT Press.

Strawson, P. (1959). *Individuals*. London: Methuen.

Strawson, P. (1974). *Freedom and resentment and other essays*. London: Methuen.

Thompson, E., & Varela, F. (2001). Radical embodiment: Neural dynamics and consciousness. *Trends in Cognitive Science, 5*(10), 416–425.

Tomasello, M. (1999). *The cultural origins of human cognition*. Cambridge, MA: Harvard University Press.

Tomasello, M. (2014). *The natural history of human thinking*. Cambridge, MA: Harvard University Press.

Treisman, A. (1996). The binding problem. *Current Opinion in Neurobiology, 6*, 171–178.

Trevarthen, C., & Aitken, K. (2001). Infant intersubjectivity: Research, theory and clinical applications *J. Child Psychology and Psychiatry, 42*(1), 3–41.

Tye, M. (1999). Phenomenal consciousness: The explanatory gap as a cognitive illusion. *Mind, 108*, 705–726.

Uhlhaas, P., & Singer, W. (2006). Neural synchrony in brain disorders: Relevance for cognitive dysfunctions and psychopathology. *Neuron, 52*, 155–168.

Vallacher, R. R., & Wegner, D. M. (1985). *A theory of action identification*. Hove: Lawrence Ehrlbaum & Associates.

Van Fraasen, B. (2008). *Scientific representation: Paradoxes of perspective*. Oxford: Oxford University Press.

Van Orden, G., Pennington, B., & Stone, G. (2001). What do double dissociations prove? *Cognitive Science, 25*, 111–172.

Vygotsky, L. (1978). *Mind in society*. Boston: Harvard University Press.

Vygotsky, L. S. (1962 [1929]). *Thought and language* (E. Hanfmann & G. Vakar, Trans.). Cambridge, MA: MIT Press.

Wegner, D. (2002). *The illusion of the conscious will*. Cambridge, MA: MIT Press.

Weiscrantz, L. (1997). *Consciousness lost and found*. Oxford: Oxford University Press.

Weitz, M. (1956). The role of theory in aesthetics. *Journal of Aesthetics and Art Criticism, 15*, 27–35.

Whiteside, S., Port, J., & Abramovitz, J. (2004). A meta-analysis of functional neuroimaging in obsessive-compulsive disorder. *Psychiatry Research: Neuroimaging, 132*, 69–79.

Williams, B. (1985). *Ethics and the limits of philosophy*. London: Fontana.

Winch, P. (1958). *The idea of a social science and its relation to philosophy*. London: Routledge.

Wittgenstein, L. (1922). *Tractatus logico philosophicus* (D. Pears & B. McGuiness, Trans.). London: Routledge & Kegan Paul. Remarks are referred to by number: thus e.g. 5.453.

Wittgenstein, L. (1953). *Philosophical investigations* (G. E. M. Anscombe, Trans.). Oxford: Blackwell (hereinafter PI with paragraphs referred to by #nn, and English pages as 232e).

Wittgenstein, L. (1965). Wittgenstein's lecture on ethics. *Philosophical Review, 74*, 3–26.

Wittgenstein, L. (1967). *Zettel* (G. E. M. Anscombe, Trans., G. E. M. Anscombe & G. H. von Wright, Eds.). Oxford: Basil Blackwell (hereinafter Z with paragraphs referred to by #nn).

Wittgenstein, L. (1969). *On certainty* (G. E. M. Anscombe & G. H. von Wright, Eds.). New York: Harper

Wittgenstein, L. (1975). *Philosophical remarks* (R. Hargreaves & R. White, Eds.). Oxford: Blackwell.

Wollheim, R. (1970). *Art and its objects*. London: Penguin.

Wood, A. (2003). Kant and the problem of human nature. In B. Jacobs & P. Kain (Eds.), *Essays on Kant's anthropology*. Cambridge: Cambridge University Press.

Young, L., Dodell-Feder, D., & Saxe, R. (2010). Who gets the attention of the temporo-parietal junction? Am fMRI investigation of attention and theory of mind. *Neuropsychologia, 48*, 2658–2664.

Zahavi, D. (2003). *Husserl's phenomenology*. Stanford, CA: Stanford University Press.

Zahavi, D. (2005). *Subjectivity and selfhood: Investigating the first person perspective.* Cambridge, MA: MIT Press.

Zahavi, D. (2013) Intentionality and phenomenology: Phenomenological take on the hard problem. *Canadian Journal of Philosophy* 32 (Suppl) 63-92.

Zeki, S. (1998). Art and the brain. *Daedalus, 127,* 71–103.

Zhu, J. (2004). Locating volition. *Consciousness and Cognition, 13,* 302–322.

Ziff, P. (1953). The task of defining a work of art. *Philosophical Review, 62*(1), 58–78.

# Index[1]

[1] Note: Page numbers followed by 'n' refer to notes.

© The Author(s) 2018
G. Gillett, *From Aristotle to Cognitive Neuroscience*,
https://doi.org/10.1007/978-3-319-93635-2